A HISTORY OF WATER SUPPLY IN LINCOLNSHIRE

GRANTHAM

Eric D. Newton

Published by
THE SOCIETY FOR LINCOLNSHIRE HISTORY AND ARCHAEOLOGY
2024

Preface and Acknowledgments

As a water engineer, I was directly involved with redevelopment work at Saltersford and other associated water supply projects in the Grantham area during the 1970s and 1980s when I was employed by Anglian Water. During that period I was employed as Engineering Projects Manager and Team Leader for the design, construction and commissioning of many water supply projects throughout Lincolnshire and South Humberside. The redevelopment of the Saltersford Treatment Plant and Pumping Station was one of the major projects. I was also responsible for the regular inspections and safety of the dams on the Cringle Brook.

During the course of the project at Saltersford I learnt much of the history surrounding the site and also noted the archaeological work undertaken by Henry Preston, the Waterworks Company's Manager during the late 1800s and early 1900s. I must also mention Ian Smith, a colleague who began work for the Grantham Waterworks Company in 1938, became Engineer and Manager to the Kesteven Water Board from 1961 to 1974 and retired from Anglian Water in 1981. He died in 2012 at the age of 96 widely known as 'Mr Waterworks'. Perhaps this book should be dedicated to the memory of Ian Smith.

In the preparation of this book I have relied much on information that I collected and photographs I took whilst employed at Anglian Water. The centenary booklet prepared by the former Grantham Waterworks Company in 1949 has also been a valuable source of material. The Lincolnshire Museum's Information Sheet (Archaeological Series No. 9) has provided details of the piped system supplying the Conduit House during the pre-1850 period. Other factual information has been retrieved from the 'Engineering 100 Returns' prepared by Anglian Water for the Kesteven Area in 1980 and from the websites of the British Newspaper Archives, the National Library of Scotland, and the British Geological Society.

I am a civil engineer by profession and therefore my writing has a strong bias to the technical rather than the financial aspects of the development of the Grantham's water supply system. Finally, being now retired, I must emphasise that my comments do not necessarily reflect the views and policies of Anglian Water Services Ltd, the current provider of public water supplies for the Grantham area.

Eric Newton CEng. MICE, January 2021

Introduction

Although artefacts have been found dating back to the Neolithic period, the town of Grantham was first properly settled during Saxon times, initially as a small village on the banks of the upper Witham, with the river and nearby springs providing a good clean water supply to the inhabitants. However, prior to the Saxons, a Romano-British settlement is known to have existed at Saltersford, approximately two miles to the south of Grantham and where the old Salters' Road from Droitwich in Worcestershire, crossed the River Witham on the way to the Lincolnshire coast. The settlement is thought to have been called *Causennae* and to have covered a sizable area. Much has been written on the Roman town at Saltersford and many Roman objects are displayed at the Grantham Museum[1].

By the eleventh century, Grantham had grown into a market town for the surrounding area and had a population of around 1,000. During the thirteenth century, the Franciscan friars, known as the Greyfriars, established a priory in Grantham. With its main export being wool, the town continued to grow during the Middle Ages, receiving its first Royal Charter in 1463. The friars established their own private water supply, piped to the friary from a local spring west of the town. Following the dissolution of the monasteries in the 1530s the friars' water supply was appropriated by the town and a public conduit house, still standing, was erected in the Market Place in 1597. Situated on the Great North Road from London, Grantham became a busy staging post and continued to be an important and prosperous market town.

During the early part of the nineteenth century, a number of engineering industries were set up in Grantham, manufacturing predominantly agricultural machinery. In 1850 the railways arrived and, with the expansion of the town's engineering works and foundries, Grantham became known as an engineering town. The main works were those of Richard Hornsby and Sons, which were located at Spittlegate. The company originally built steam engines but after the turn of the century, went on to manufacture oil and gas engines. They initiated work on the steerable caterpillar track, which was used on the new tanks in World War One.

The town gained gas light in 1832, to be followed by its first piped water supply in 1850. Grantham Town Hall was built in 1869 and a hospital opened in 1874. By the

---

[1] Grantham Museum is located on St Peter's Hill in the town centre. Founded by Henry Preston in the early twentieth century, it is run by the Grantham Community Heritage Association.

mid-1800s, the town's population was around 11,000, rising to over 16,000 by the end of the century.[2]

During the twentieth century, Grantham continued to grow, with engineering being its main industrial base. The Depression of the early 1930s badly affected the engineering industries within the town, although these were revived with the onset of World War Two. With large armaments works being located in Grantham, the town was heavily bombed during the war. Following the end of hostilities, Grantham prospered again, but only until the 1970s, after which many of the engineering works closed. Nevertheless, the town's population continued to grow with the establishment of food processing companies and many smaller businesses. By the end of the twentieth century the town's population stood at approximately 40,000[3].

Topography, Geology and Water Resources

Grantham sits in the valley of the upper reaches of the River Witham which has its source some ten miles to the south near the village of South Witham. From its source the river flows due north following its valley and through the centre of Grantham before continuing in a northerly direction for another twenty miles to Lincoln. The gently rolling landscape to the south and west of the town is crossed by the Cringle Brook which flows through Stoke Rochford Park to join the Witham from the west, approximately four miles upstream of Grantham.

To the north, the topography of the land levels out across the Witham and Trent valleys. Immediately to the east, however, the land rises up sharply to the limestone escarpment of the Lincolnshire Ridge that runs due north-south up the length of the county. To the east of the ridge are the gently dipping limestone heathlands.

The surface geology of the area to the south of Grantham and west of the River Witham is predominantly that of the Jurassic limestones overlaid in part by boulder clay where the limestones have suffered much erosion due to glaciation. The limestones in turn overlie a thin layer of estuarine clays and sands, below which is found a seam of the Northampton ironstones. These have been quarried and exploited extensively west of the Witham between Denton and Cottesmore as well as further south towards Corby.

---

[2] Page, William (Ed), *Victoria County History: Lincolnshire,* Volume 2, 1906.
[3] Data on current population taken from City Population website.

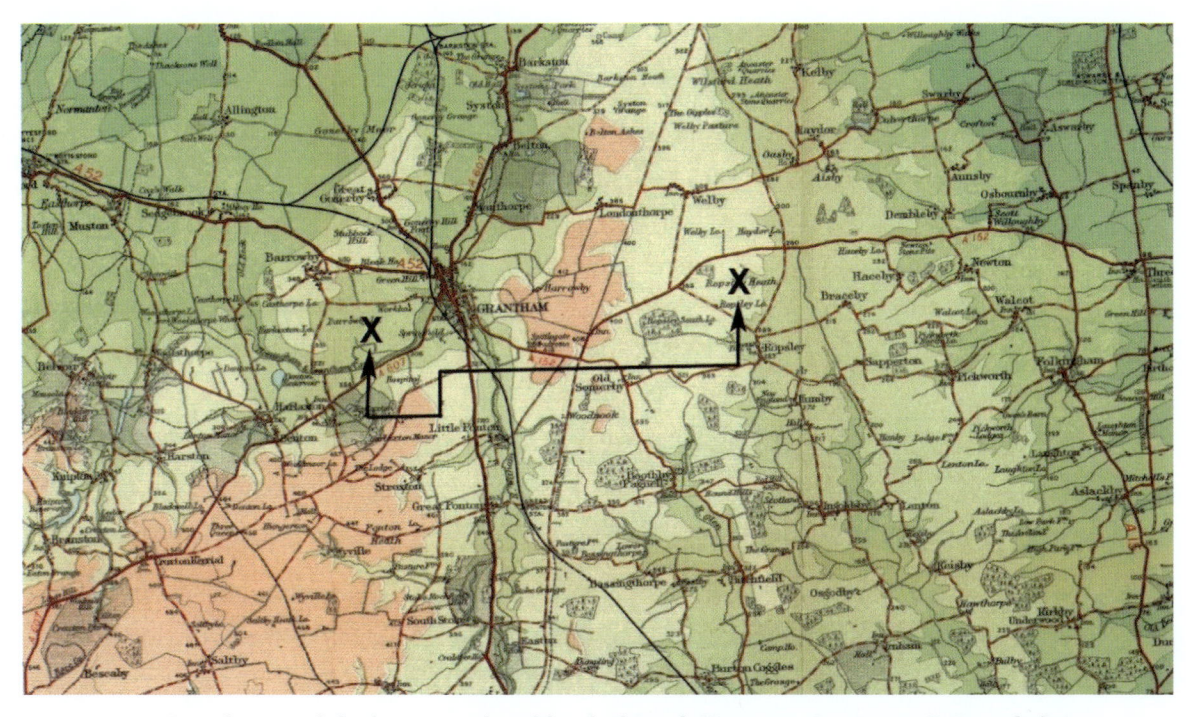

Grantham and the limestone heathland of South Kesteven. Section at X-X, see below.

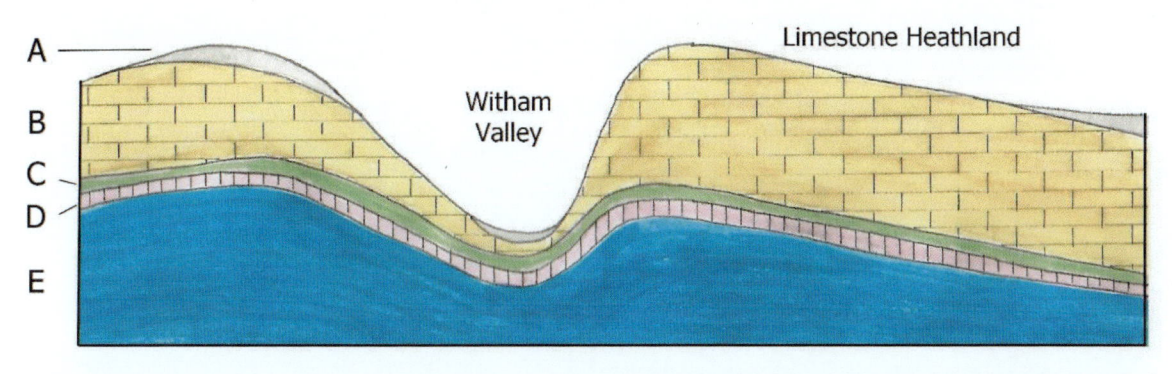

Section X-X across the limestone heathland and the Witham valley south of Grantham, vertical scale exaggerated. (A – Boulder Clay; B – Lincolnshire Limestone; C – Estuarine Sands and Gravels; D – Northamptonshire Ironstone; E – Lias Clays.)

Below the ironstones lie the blue Lias clays of the Lower Jurassic period. Data obtained from boreholes drilled in the area to the south of Grantham indicate that some folding of the strata layers has occurred, resulting in a dip that now forms the valley of the upper Witham before rising sharply to create the limestone escarpment immediately to the east of the river.[4]

From the top of the limestone escarpment the sequence of the geological formations to the west of the Witham dip gently eastwards. In the central town area there is a nine-metre depth of sands and gravels that formed an ancient river bed above a layer of stiff grey clay.

Within the limestones are thin bands of clay, immediately above which many springs emerge. These are found principally along the banks of the River Witham and Cringle Brook and also in feeding the Wyville Beck, which is a tributary of the Cringle Brook. In addition, there are spots where the limestone groundwater bubbles up to the surface under artesian head through the overlying boulder clay, for example at Stroxton, which then flows direct to the River Witham at Little Ponton.

On the bankside of the River Witham, in the vicinity of Great and Little Ponton in particular, emerges a number of free-flowing springs, from which under normal conditions there is a constant flow of water from the limestones. One such spring is Bath Spring where sometime in the past a small stone octagonal bathing pool was constructed with steps leading down into the pool. This still exists.

Bath Spring, close to the east bank of the River Witham at Little Ponton, (SK 927327).

---

[4] British Geological Survey, https://www.bgs.ac.uk, for details of onshore borehole scans.

In past years a series of dams have been constructed along the courses of both the Cringle Brook and Wyville Beck to form lakes, mainly for recreational use but also to provide local storage for milling and water supply. The system is explained in more detail in the next chapter, including the 'waterfall' at Stoke Rochford.

The combined waters of the River Witham, Cringle and Wyville brooks have been utilised for a number of purposes, not least to power mills along the Witham upstream and downstream of Grantham. It was the mill owners that raised objections during the late nineteenth century and early twentieth century against the abstraction of water from the River Witham and its tributaries for public water supply purposes.

The Cringle Brook and Wyville Beck

The source of the Cringle Brook is near the village of Buckminster and flows some 8 miles in a northerly direction through Skillington and Stoke Rochford Park, then under the A1 highway (Great North Road) to join the River Witham just upstream of Great Ponton. The Wyville Beck emanates from a spring at the hamlet of Wyville, flowing eastwards for 2½ miles past Home Farm to join the Cringle Brook within the grounds of Stoke Rochford Park.

Stoke Rochford Hall, home of the Turnor family. The artificial lake (Top Lake) in the foreground is fed by the Cringle Brook.

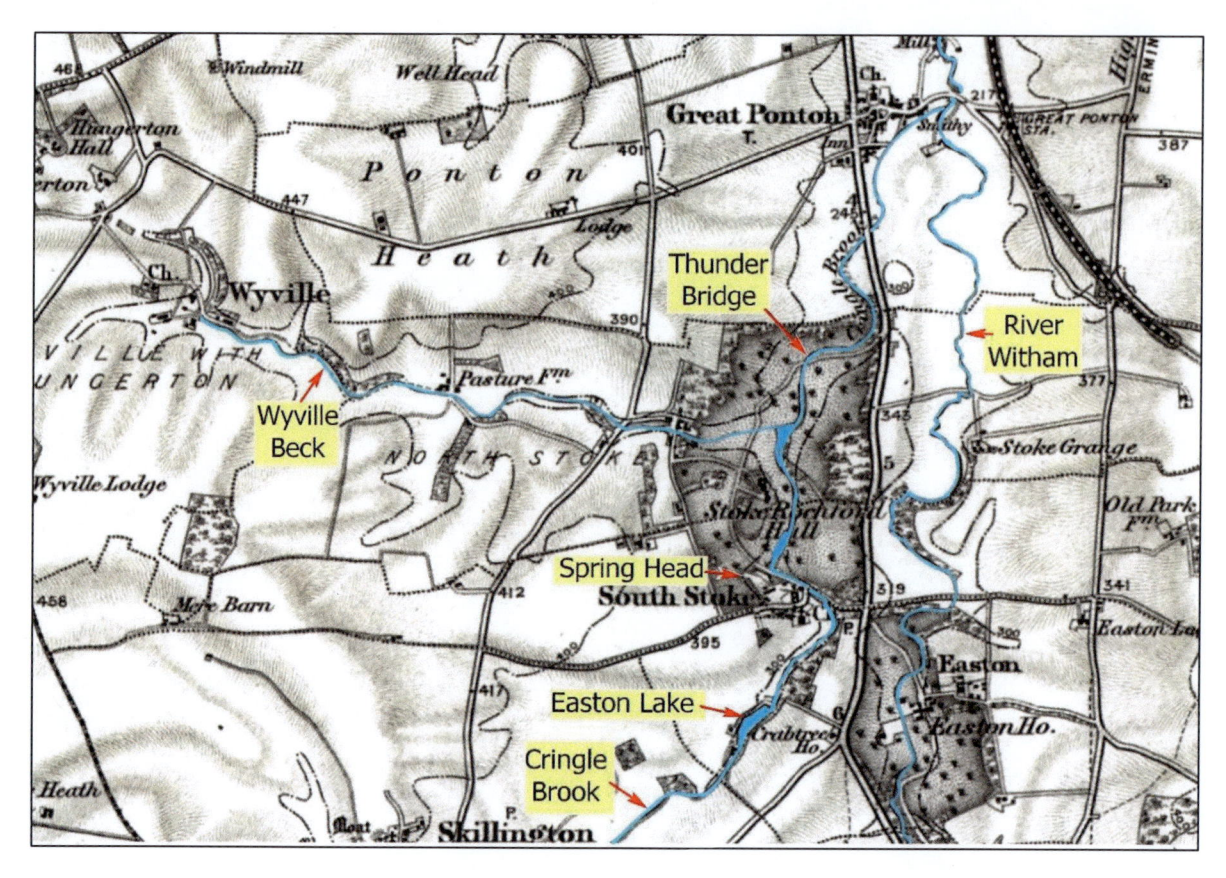

Watercourses south of Grantham.

Numerous springs from the limestones discharge into these two watercourses and supplement their flows before they discharge into the Witham. In past years a number of these springs have been tapped by the installation of pumping plant to supply some of the local villages, farmsteads and Stoke Rochford Hall. However, with the coming of public piped water supplies, virtually all these local arrangements are now redundant.

One of the largest springs is at Spring Head, which is located on a bankside within the grounds of Stoke Rochford Hall. In 1661 Bishop Sanderson described the spring as 'from the side of the hill, winning the admiration of the divine, flowed a goodly spring of clear water, issuing out in such abundance that it turneth an ancient mill immediately at the mouth thereof"[5]. There are now no signs of the 'ancient mill', but an artificial waterfall has been created immediately downstream, creating a drop of up to 3.5 metres (12 feet) which, during times of high discharge from the spring, produces a spectacular sight.[6]

Along the watercourses of the Cringle Brook and Wyville Beck there are fifteen large lakes and ponds, of which four are along the Wyville Beck. Most are man-made by the construction of dams and weirs and include the lake formed partially by the embankment of the A1 highway. Of the fifteen lakes and ponds, four have substantial earth dams that impound waters to form some of the larger lakes. With one exception, they were all constructed for amenity and recreational purposes such as boating and fishing during the eighteenth and nineteenth centuries. The three lakes immediately below Stoke Rochford Hall are good examples of this. Similarly, the grassed embankment dam further upstream at Easton created a lake for the residents of Easton Hall on the opposite side of the A1 highway.

Waterfall at Spring Head, 2012 (SK 917275).

The one exception to recreational use is on the Wyville Beck at Home Farm where the stored water was used to power the local mill. At Stoke Rochford the attractive concrete dam at Thunder Bridge across the Lower Lake, where water cascades down its downstream face, was later rebuilt to regulate water supplies to the water treatment works at Saltersford. Together with the gently rolling countryside and the waterfall at Spring Head, the area could be described as 'the mini lake district of Lincolnshire'. It is indeed an attractive area.

---

[5] Terence R Leach, 1978, *Notes for the visit to Stoke Rochford and Easton,* Society for Lincolnshire History and Archaeology.
[6] Eric D Newton, 'A Lincolnshire Waterfall?', *Lincolnshire Past & Present*, **91**, 2013, pp. 3-5.

Thunder Bridge Dam on Cringle Brook, one of the attractive water features in and around Stoke Rochford.

Early Water Supplies:
Roman Period to Mid-Nineteenth Century

There has been a sizable settlement at Grantham dating back to the Neolithic period. Situated on the upper Witham, which is fed from spring sources to the south of the town, there has always been an adequate supply of water available to the local inhabitants. Water would also have been taken from the many springs in the immediate locality of the town together with that abstracted from private wells sunk into the river gravels.

At the time of the Roman occupation, an ample and good quality supply of water would have been required to meet the high standards of hygiene for their settlement at Saltersford, thought to be *Causennae*. This was readily available from the upper Witham and nearby springs. The population of the Roman settlement is unknown but from the area occupied it would have been of a reasonable size. From archaeological investigations at the site, a three-metre deep well was discovered alongside the river. Also, on the sloping bankside to the west, drainage channels were exposed which led to a stone tank. It is a matter of speculation how the Romans abstracted water from the well and how it was conveyed to the various distribution points around the settlement.

The Romans were innovative water engineers and from evidence found elsewhere throughout their empire, they were adept at lifting water from lower levels to cisterns and fountains for collection. Other than the well and drainage channels, no other evidence relating to a Roman water supply system has to date been found at Saltersford, although other permanent works must have existed. Sadly, none have survived.

During the Saxon and early Norman periods within the settlement of Grantham, water supplies would have continued to be drawn from local wells and collected from nearby springs. The quality of the water taken from the springs would have been good for drinking but would have needed to be carried or carted some distance to people's homes. That taken from some of the shallow wells, however, would probably have been polluted from the discharge of household sewage into nearby cesspits.

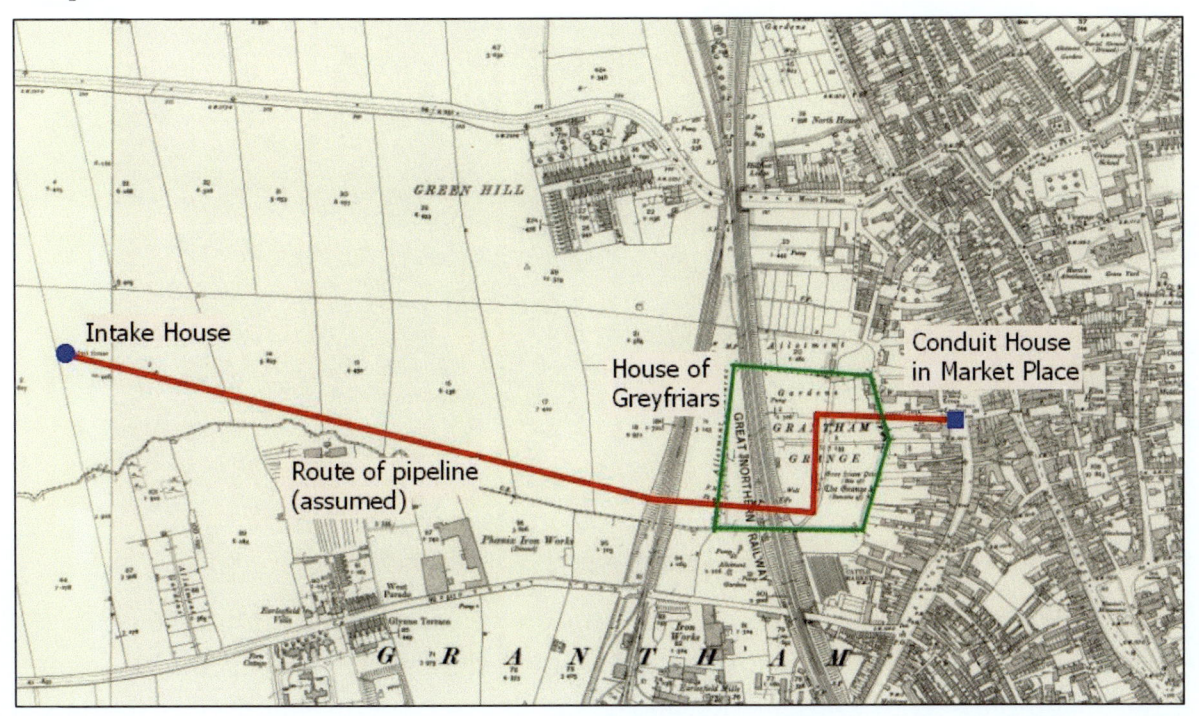

Plan of Spring Supply to Conduit House.

Perhaps the first real evidence of a piped water supply was during the early fourteenth century when in 1314 the Greyfriars, whose priory was located on the present-day site of The Grange, obtained permission to lay lead pipes from a spring half a mile to the west of the town.[7] The spring, which still flows, is located in a field between Dysart Road and the A52 Barrowby Road, where a small stone building known as the Intake House was constructed over the spring. The building was fully restored in 1930 but has since been vandalised and almost totally destroyed. The lead pipeline from the spring is thought to have then followed the Barrowby Beck to the 'House of the Greyfriars'.

After the Dissolution of the Monasteries in the 1530s, the property of the Greyfriars passed into the private ownership of a member of Henry VIII's court who, so it would seem, subsequently allowed the Town Corporation to connect into the lead pipeline to provide a water supply for the public. The location of the Intake House at the spring and the assumed route of the pipeline, are shown above.

The Conduit House, Market Place, Grantham.

In 1597 the Corporation constructed a masonry *castelle* or Conduit House in the Market Place, from which the public could draw their water supplies. The Conduit House, complete with battlements and eight pinnacles, still stands in the Market Place and is a Scheduled Ancient Monument. Its dimensions are 13ft x 10ft with a height of 9ft to the drip course that defines the level of the roof. Inside the masonry building is a cistern or storage tank which supplied a faucet on the east side of the

---

[7] Romano-British Settlement, Saltersford, see Lincolnshire Heritage Explorer, https://heritage-explorer.lincolnshire,gov.uk/Monument/MLI33968.

Conduit House from which water would have been drawn. Around the four sides of the Conduit House there are a number of inscriptions, mainly of the names of prominent persons in the town, but above the drinking fountain is inscribed 'Let thy fountains be dispersed abroad and rivers of waters in the street', a biblical quotation from Proverbs and probably a feature of the original 1597 masonry structure. The Conduit House remained in use until the mid-1800s when the faucet was removed and replaced with the drinking fountain in 1860.[8]

Throughout its 250 years in use as the town's main source of drinking water, the Conduit House and pipeline required many repairs and much maintenance. During the 1600s it is recorded that a Keeper of the Conduit was employed with a salary of 30 shillings per annum. Fines were imposed against anyone who should 'annoy the Conduitt by rinseing or washing of clothes or doeing other business there to prejudice the Conduitt'. There is also an account of watercarts being rented by private individuals for the delivery of drinking water from the Conduit House to people's homes. A rent of £3/0/0 per annum was paid to the Corporation 'provided that no other persons do goe with any water-carts'. A detailed account of Grantham's Conduit is given in the Lincolnshire Museums' Information Sheet – Archaeological Series No 9, from which much of the above information was obtained.

Stroxton Springs and Spittlegate Reservoir, 1850s

By the mid-nineteenth century the population of Grantham was about 11,000 and growing rapidly due in part to the arrival of the Great Northern Railway's main-line from London to Doncaster and the setting up of the new engineering industries within the town, manufacturing mainly agricultural machinery. As a result, the demand for a good quality piped water supply was growing. Very few had water piped to their own homes but it had to be carted from the conduit house or nearby springs and wells. Some of the larger houses had hand-pumps in the kitchens that were connected to soft water cisterns under the floors which in turn were fed by rainwater collected from roofs.[9] However, after a relatively short period in storage, this roof-water became foul and unsuitable for use.

---

[8] Lincolnshire Museums, Information Sheet, Archaeological Series, Sheet No. 9.
[9] 'Centenary of the Grantham Waterworks Company, 1849 -1949', Booklet.

SUPPLY OF PURE WATER.

TO THE MAYOR, OF GRANTHAM.

We, the undersigned, do hereby request you to call a PUBLIC MEETING of the Inhabitants of the Borough and Hamlets, for the purpose of taking into consideration a Scheme for the supply of Water to all classes, at a high pressure; and adopting such measures thereon, as may be thought desirable.

17th October, 1849.

John Garnar	Thomas Ekin
Richd. Briggs	W. Dixon
W. Walkington	George Smith
Wm. Watson	Wm. G. Wagstaffe
Henry Pearce	Jos. J. A. Brown
E. M. Rogers	Thos. Howison
Chas. Jas. Windover	Thos. Burgess
Robt. Brewster	Jabez Thompson
Samuel Bryan	W. Ostler, Junr.
Herbert King	Tho. Bushby
Edwd. Bond	C. G. Gray
Joseph Hancock	Wm. Swain
Henry Thompson	George Dawson
Samuel Ridge	Richd. Gamble
Robt. Shipman	W. B. Howitt
Jno. P. King	J. Hawkins
J. Cooper	John Hardwick, Junr.
T. G. Hull	Charles Lord
Gabriel Pigott	William Aldridge
F. Brindley	William Pick
Thos. Hopkinson	L. Wyles, Junr.
John Bailey	Wyles & Booth
Thomas Harvey	Josh. Hind
E. L. Hough	John Walker
William Robbs	Thos. Winter

In compliance with the above Requisition, I hereby appoint a Public Meeting of the Inhabitants of Grantham and the Hamlets, to be held at the GUILDHALL, on TUESDAY, the 23rd day of October Instant, at Ten o'Clock.

SIGNED.

ROBT. MATHER,
MAYOR.

RIDGE, PRINTER, GRANTHAM.

Notice of a Public meeting to be held on 23 October 1849 to discuss Grantham's Water Supply.

A request was submitted to the mayor from 50 signatories to consider 'a Scheme for the supply of Water to all classes, at a high pressure, and adopting such measures thereon, as may be thought desirable'. As a result, a public meeting was called on the 23 October 1849 in the town's Guildhall to discuss the issue of a new water supply The outcome of the meeting was the setting up of a private water company with shares issued to raise sufficient capital for a scheme of works to be implemented which would provide the town with a new water supply, as set out in the Waterworks Clauses Act 1847.[10] The new Grantham Waterworks Company was registered in 1850 with the task of appointing an engineer to find a new source of water and to prepare a scheme to provide the townsfolk of Grantham with a satisfactory water supply.

George Meredith, who originated from Dublin, was duly appointed as engineer for 'the design and to superintend the execution' of the necessary works. Thanks to the generosity of the local landowner Sir Glynne Welby, abstraction rights were granted to the company to take water from three springs, one of which was Church Spring, in the vicinity of Stroxton Village, approximately three miles south of the town.[11]

A gravity-fed pipeline using earthenware pipes was laid to an underground covered service reservoir constructed near the top of Spittlegate Hill to the south of the town centre and alongside London Road. The reservoir was built in engineering brickwork with a concrete base. From the reservoir an 8-inch diameter pipeline was laid down into the town to supply the network of pipes feeding homes and various collection points.

At the outset numerous objections were lodged to the use of the springs at Stroxton, especially from the mill-owners on the River Witham downstream of Little Ponton; they were concerned about potentially reduced flows in the river. Terms of compensation were eventually settled and the works providing a new water supply to the townsfolk was completed by February 1851.[12] It can be assumed that the settlement of the objections received from the mill-owners did not deter progress of the new water supply project. No doubt the inhabitants of Grantham, together with the newly arrived railway, were putting pressure on the company to complete the

---

[10] Waterworks Clauses Act 1847. This Act gave powers and laid down conditions for the abstraction of water and construction of works to provide water supplies. It also made clear how undertakers could charge for work and supply water; it also introduced penalties for the misuse of water and non-payment.
[11] Work at Stroxton carried out under the powers of the Waterworks Clauses Act 1847.
[12] Waterworks Company, Centenary booklet.

project. It seems that the service reservoir was constructed in stages as the completion of 'five additional chambers' is recorded in 1869 with another yet to be added. This would make a total of eight chambers in all, giving an overall capacity of 800,000 gallons.

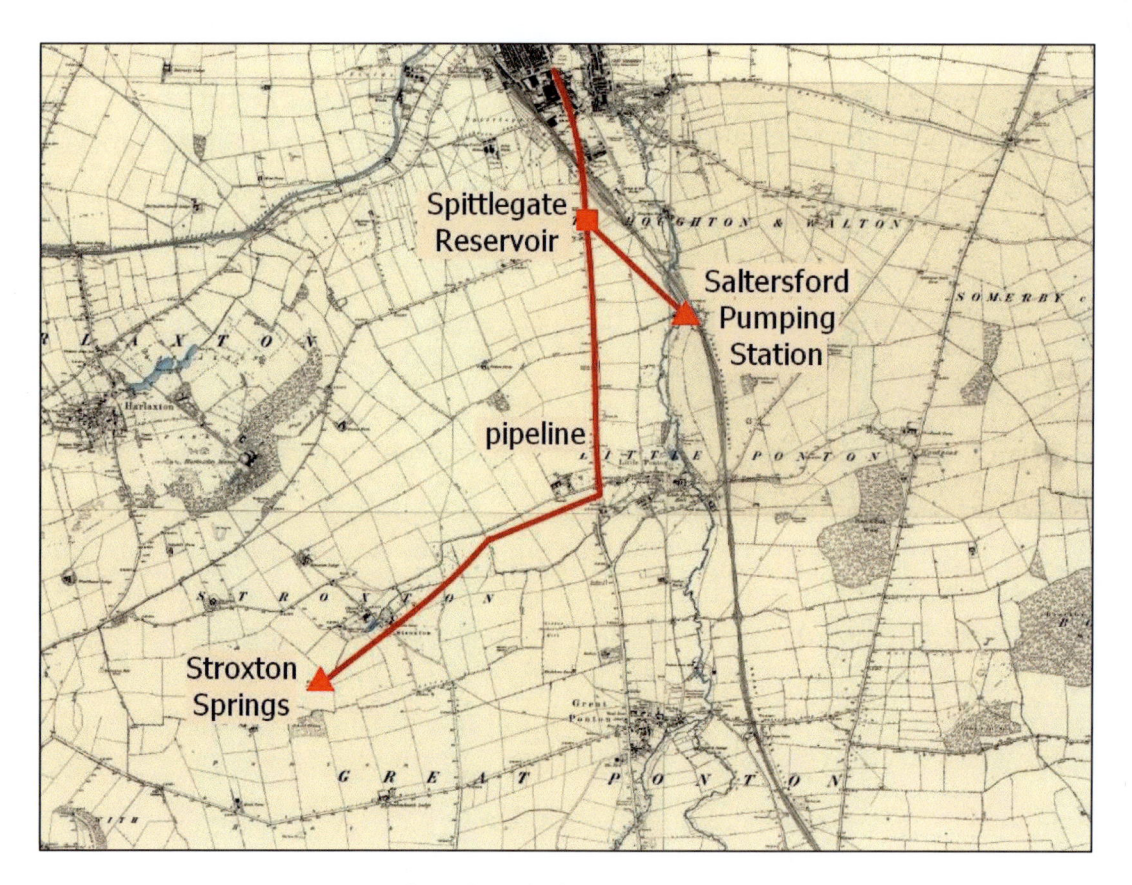

Plan of supply from Stroxton Springs.

However, the low and unreliable yields from the springs at Stroxton during the summer months were soon found to be insufficient to meet the demands of the town's population. Horizontal adits below ground level were dug into the limestones to increase the yields from two springs and a steam-driven pump was installed. In addition, the leaking earthenware pipes to the reservoir on Spittlegate improvements, the quantity of water that could reliably be abstracted at Stroxton during the dry periods was still insufficient to meet the town's ever-growing demands. There were also problems of water quality at times of low flows from the springs and it soon became apparent that an additional source of water was needed.

Interior of Spittlegate Reservoir.

Saltersford Pumping Station and Cringle Brook, 1858 to 1900

In 1858, once again with much opposition from the mill-owners, the Waterworks Company started to acquire the rights to abstract water from four springs alongside the River Witham in the parishes of Great and Little Ponton, from which water was to be piped direct to a new pumping station constructed downstream at Saltersford. Included was the previously mentioned Bath Spring together with Swamp Spring and Hovel Spring. Saltersford, being on the site of what is thought to be the Roman settlement of *Causennae*, is also on the northern boundary of Little Ponton parish and was chosen as being the furthest point away from any housing within the parish, especially Little Ponton Hall. It is in any event a most suitable site, with a levelled area on both sides of the river and reasonably close to the reservoir at Spittlegate. A pumphouse was constructed at Saltersford with steam operated pumping plant installed to pump up to 50,000 gallons/day via a new pipeline laid up to the service reservoir at Spittlegate.

The main source of water to the town was still being supplied by gravity from the springs at Stroxton, while water from the Ponton springs was pumped from Saltersford and used mainly to supply the Great Northern Railway and other industrial users. In 1871 it was reported that the pipeline from Stroxton was extended to collect from four extra springs and brought down to Saltersford.[13]

Spring near Little Ponton.

However, the demands for water continued to grow as the town's population further increased. Advice was required by the Waterworks Company about the works necessary to meet these increasing needs. In 1868 Mr Haywood, Engineer to the Corporation of London, was consulted and he subsequently produced a comprehensive report for consideration. The recommendations were that the company obtain the rights to take water from the Cringle Brook which flows through Stoke Rochford Park.

The plan was to construct a dam and intake works on the brook to the east of the Great North Road, prior to its discharge into the Witham at Great Ponton. From the intake a pipeline would be laid direct to the Saltersford Works. At Saltersford, a bankside reservoir was to be constructed and new pumps installed. The recommendations were accepted by the company, but new capital funds needed to be raised. Christopher Turnor, the landowner of Stoke Rochford Park, through which the Cringle Brook passed, raised no objections to the taking of water from the brook, but there were many objections from the mill-owners on the Witham downstream of Ponton.

---

[13] *Grantham Journal (hereafter abbreviated as GJ)*, 27 May 1871.

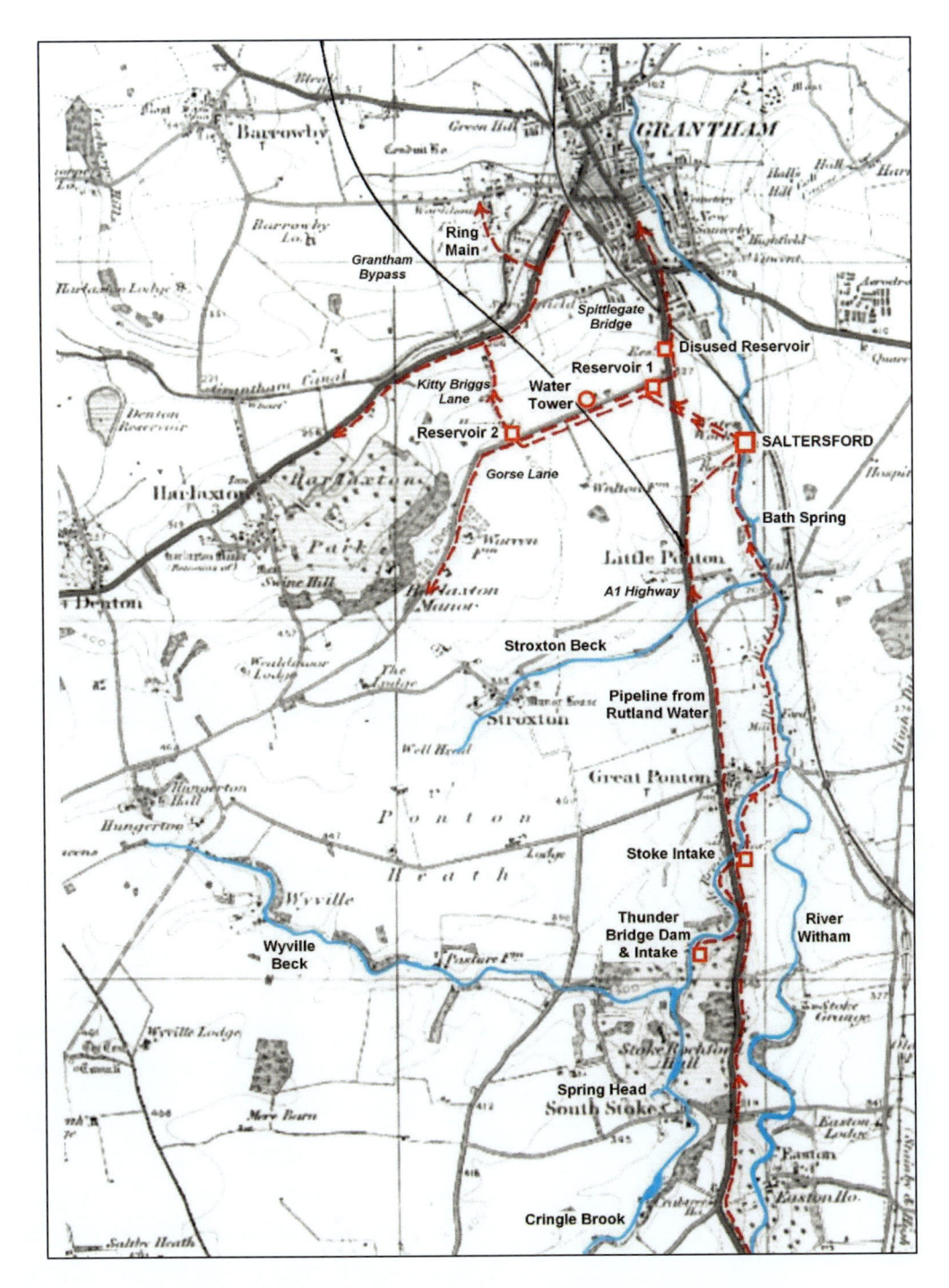

Grantham water supplies to and from Saltersford Pumping Station.

To be able to undertake and finance the new work, new powers and additional capital were required. In 1873 the company sought and obtained its first Act of Parliament.[14] Under this Act, the pioneer Waterworks Company was dissolved and re-incorporated into the newly formed 'Grantham Waterworks Company' with the usual statutory powers and obligations that were customary for other water companies in England at that time.

The Act, known as the 'Grantham Waterworks Act 1873', granted the new company the powers 'to acquire land, to take water from the Cringle Brook to supply the inhabitants of Grantham and to construct the necessary works'. In addition, the share capital was raised to £25,000 with the powers to raise further capital.

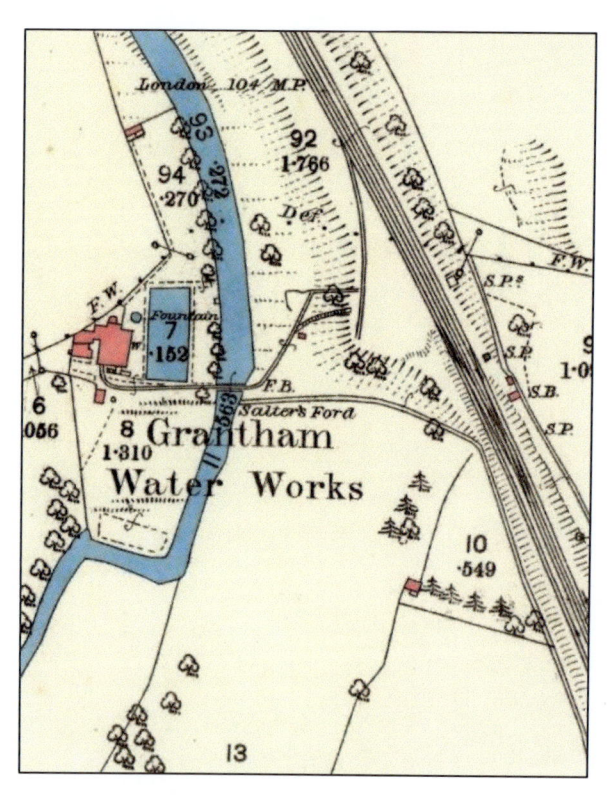

Work soon commenced. Where the brook emerges from the tunnel under the Great North Road at Stoke Bridge, an intake complex was constructed, complete with roughening filters and settling tanks. From the intake a pipeline was laid direct to Saltersford Pumping Station where an open reservoir was built to provide storage before pumping up to Spittlegate Hill. The reservoir with a capacity of 400,000 gallons was constructed with mass concrete walls lined with blue engineering brick. To accommodate the reservoir and pumphouse in the limited space available, it was necessary to make a small diversion of the river as shown in the map to the left.

Saltersford Pumping Station, 1885. Extract from Ordnance Survey County Series, 1:2500.

A new steam-operated pump was initially installed on the east side of the river; this was a small 20 horsepower 'Grasshopper' type beam engine complete

---

[14] The Grantham Waterworks Act, 1873. This dissolved the pioneering company and established the new Grantham Waterworks Company, which had powers to abstract water from the Cringle Brook, to construct works, to raise capital and to make charges.

with boiler and pump. However, after only twelve months, a major overhaul was required and, because the output was insufficient to meet the ever-increasing demands, a new and larger pump was needed. As a consequence, in 1876 a large 51/70 HP 'condensing' steam-driven beam engine and pump, manufactured by The Perran Foundry of Perranporth, Cornwall, was installed on the west side of the river.[15]

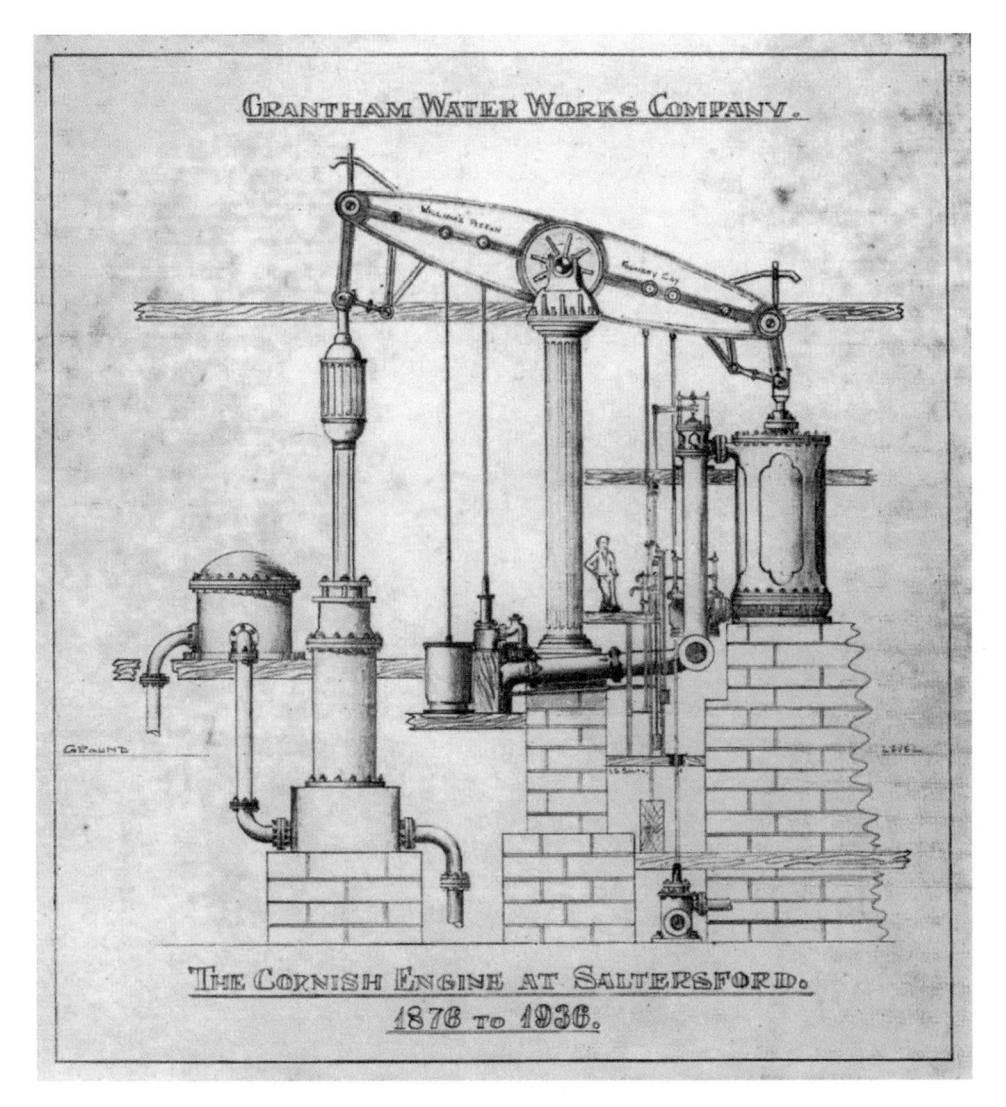

The Cornish Engine at Saltersford, from the Centenary Booklet, 1949.

---

[15] *GJ*, 5 August 1876.

Powered by twin Cornish boilers, the engine was initially capable of pumping up to 34,000 gph and later increased to the 40,000 gph following fitting of a new and larger pump in 1897. A purpose-built pump-house, 60 feet tall, was constructed in red brick with stone facings, with a brick chimneystack serving the boilers. The cost of the steam-driven pumping engine and building installed in 1876 was £4,120.[16]

Saltersford pumphouse in 1876.

Although the 'Cornishman' performed well, it did break down for a four-week period in 1883.[17] Because there was no suitable standby available, the town had to rely on a much-reduced supply from the Stroxton springs, which did create some problems, not least for the railways. As a result, a new steam operated pump unit from Tangyes Ltd of Birmingham was purchased in 1883 and installed in a new building on the east side of the river. This pump unit was capable of delivering 16,000 gallons per hour (gph), which, together with the Grasshopper engine, would provide standby to the 'Cornishman' when it was being maintained and out of service. In 1879 the average daily amount of water supplied by the company was 580,000 gallons.[18]

---

[16] Centenary Booklet. The Cornish beam engine & pump cost £2,120; the pumphouse building £ 2,000.
[17] Clifford Dack, *Grantham Waterworks Company*.
[18] *GJ*, 6 February 1909.

From the old Ordnance Survey map of 1885, it is interesting to note that the railway embankment that carries the main East Coast railway line above the treatment works was widened to accommodate a small siding. Presumably this was for railway trucks supplying coal for the steam engine's boilers. On the same map it appears that a tramway was laid down the embankment and across the river to the engine house, again presumably for transporting coal. A staircase is also shown up the side of the embankment.

The steam-driven Cornish beam engine continued to be the principal means of pumping water from Saltersford for many years and did yeoman service up to when it was finally retired and dismantled in 1936. In 1898/99 it is recorded that the Grasshopper engine was moved to the west side of the river to be with the 'Cornishman' and that a new steam-driven duplex compound engine and pump supplied by Hydraulic Engineering Co of Chester was installed alongside[19]. Known as the 'Blake Steam Pump', it was capable of pumping 50,000 gph.

Blake Steam Pump Engine at Saltersford, 1899.

---

[19] *GJ*, 6 March 1869.

With all the engines and pumps now on the west side of the river, a new Lancashire boiler in a new boiler house was installed to supply steam to all three engines to supplement the two existing Cornish boilers. The Tangyes engine on the east side of the river was retained on standby. The combined pumping capacity of the three steam-driven pumps was now 2,400,000 gallons per day (gpd), although they did not all operate together, nor indeed for 24 hours a day.

It is also recorded that water supplied by the company in 1898 had 'broken all records', due in part to the prosperity of Messrs R. Hornsby and Sons Ltd, whose engineering works was now the largest in Grantham.[20] It is worth mentioning that one of the Water Company's board members was also a director of Hornsby and Sons Ltd.

During the late nineteenth century it would seem that the company were very strict about local folk taking water illegally from their water supply system. In October 1882 it was reported in the local press that a woman who was named and described as a 'beer-house keeper' was prosecuted for illegally taking a 'can' (one gallon) of water from the company's tap in Thompson's Yard.[21] The fine was one shilling (5p) with ten shillings (50p) expenses. Similar offences were committed by others at about the same time with similar fines imposed. It was stated that a maximum fine of up to £10/0/0 could have been imposed; the company were 'were determined to put a stop to it'. It would seem that at that time clean drinking water was considered to be a precious commodity and even the smallest amount taken had to be purchased. (At today's charges the equivalent cost of one gallon of water piped direct to people's homes is around 0.7p.)

In 1898 the retirement of William Teague, engineer to the Lincoln Waterworks Company, was reported.[22] For a number of years Teague had acted as consultant engineer to the Grantham Waterworks Company and had advised the company's own engineer, Henry Preston, in the development and management of the water supply system at Grantham. The Grantham board acknowledged the technical advice given in those early years by Teague to Preston, who was not a qualified water engineer.

---

[20] *GJ*, 11 February 1899.
[21] *GJ*, 28 October 1882.
[22] *GJ*, 5 February 1898.

Henry Preston, Waterworks Manager, 1881 to 1934

Henry Preston (1852-1940) was appointed as the Manager, Secretary and Engineer to the Grantham Waterworks Company in 1881, a position he held with the company for 53 years until his retirement in 1934 at the age of 82. Born and educated in Nottingham, he received his training in geology and engineering at Manchester and at the South Kensington Royal School of Mines. He first came to Grantham in 1874 at the age of 22 as a teacher of technical subjects at evening classes, and at this early age showed much potential.

Preston started employment with the company in 1879 and within two years was promoted to manager. Based at the company's offices in Finkin Street in Grantham, as manager and engineer he oversaw and was responsible for the many changes and improvements to the water supply system for Grantham and the surrounding area over his 53 years' service. For the last six years of his life, he was employed as consultant to the Waterworks Company.[23]

However, it is perhaps as an archaeologist, historian and geologist that Preston is best known and remembered.[24] His archaeological investigations at Saltersford during the early 1900s have been well documented.[25] Prior to work commencing on the construction of the large raw-water reservoir and filters at Saltersford, he organised archaeological digs on what was thought at that time to be the location of the Roman settlement of *Causennae*. His finds were numerous, including the unearthing of stone walls and footings, paved roads and footpaths, and a well, together with tiles and many pieces

Henry Preston (1852-1940).

---

[23] *GJ*, 29 November 1940. Obituary for Henry Preston.
[24] Henry Preston, 1915, *Roman Remains at Saltersford*.
[25] Romano-British Settlement, Saltersford, Lincolnshire Heritage Explorer, Monument Record ML133968.

of pottery on both sides of the river. A large number of iron, bronze and silver artefacts were also discovered, including enamelled brooches and a hoard of coins.[26]

These discoveries established without doubt that the site at Saltersford was a Romano-British settlement and almost certainly that of *Causennae*. In addition to the Roman finds, the fossil of a plesiosaurus from pre-historic times was unearthed when excavating for the sand filters in 1914.[27]

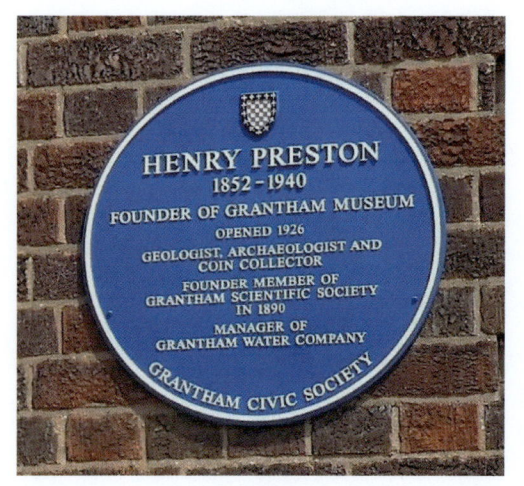

Preston was the founder of the Grantham Scientific Society in 1890 and instrumental in the establishment of the Grantham Museum in 1926, in which many of his finds from Saltersford are now on display, including his large coin collection. His portrait hangs on the wall inside the museum with a commemorative blue plaque outside on the external face of the museum building (*left*).

Saltersford Pumping Station, 1900 to late 1930s

By the turn of the century steam was giving way to oil and in 1904 a new 42 bhp Akroyd oil-driven engine, manufactured by Messrs R. Hornsby Ltd at Grantham and fitted with a Haywood Tyler pump, was installed as a back-up to the steam plant. (Hornsby are claimed to be the first company in the world to manufacture compression-ignition oil engines on a commercial basis.) The Grasshopper engine was now being used solely for pumping water from the river for washing the sand filters. In 1916 the Akroyd engine was replaced by a larger 85 bhp oil engine and pump, again supplied from Hornsby's local factory, giving an output of 45,000 gallons per hour.

This was reinforced a few years later by a second horizontal spindle pump unit with a similar output of 50,000 gph driven by a 95 bhp Ruston & Hornsby oil engine.

---

[26] Henry Preston, 1915, *Roman Remains at Saltersford*.
[27] *GJ*, 8 August 1914.

The combined pumping capacity was now raised to 95,000 gph or nearly 2,300,000 gpd.[28]

Although the Cornish beam engine was not removed until 1936, it is likely that it was only retained on a standby basis while the new and more efficient oil-driven engines and pumps were being used on a regular daily basis to supply water to the reservoir on Spittlegate Hill.

Akroyd Oil Engine, 1904.

Ruston & Hornsby Oil Engine, 1918.

By 1906 two slow sand filters, with a holding capacity of 500,000 gallons, were installed to treat water taken from the Cringle Brook, and a concrete roof was provided for the open 400,000-gallon reservoir as protection for the treated water against pollution prior to pumping. A few years later unfounded rumours were circulating about the quality of the water supplied by the company, and it was suggested that all water for drinking should be boiled.[29] However, it was rightly pointed out that the water was now filtered before passing to the covered reservoirs and that, after analysis, no dangerous or harmful bacteria were found prior to it reaching the public. The statement concluded by saying that 'it was time that they stamped out these silly scares'. During 1908 water supplied by the company had risen to 740,000 gpd of which nearly 40% was metered for industrial and commercial use.[30]

---

[28] Dack, *Grantham Waterworks Company*.
[29] *GJ*, 11 February 1911.
[30] *GJ*, 6 February 1909.

In 1909 the company needed to raise capital for improvement works to be undertaken at Saltersford and elsewhere in the system. Under the Grantham Waterworks Act 1909, powers were obtained to raise £40,000 for the construction of additional reservoir storage and filters at Saltersford and the laying of new pipelines.[31] During the years up to 1916 additional sand filters and reservoir storage were installed. A large open raw-water lagoon or settling tank of 7,250,000-gallon capacity was constructed on the east side of the river upstream of the main works on land purchased from Christopher Turnor of Stoke Rochford. This was fed by water piped direct from the Cringle Brook and passed onto the four slow sand filters installed on both sides of the river.

Re-laying the Water Main over Spittlegate Bridge, 1906.

In 1910 a Return of all water undertakings throughout England and Wales was ordered by Parliament.[32] This was published in 1914, listing areas and populations

---

[31] Grantham Waterworks Act 1909. A notice was published in Grantham Journal of 14 November 1909 announcing the powers to construct works and raise capital.
[32] Water Undertakings (England and Wales). This return to the House of Commons, dated July 1914, listed every water undertaking in England and Wales with details of powers, area supplied, sources, quantity & quality of water, population & houses supplied.

served with details of water sources and water supplied. For the Grantham Waterworks Company, the following information was given:

Powers: Grantham Waterworks Acts of 1873 and 1909

Area of supply: Grantham Borough plus parishes of Great Gonerby and Spittlegate

Population: 20,070 (1911)

Number of Houses: 4,466

Houses Supplied from Piped Services: 4,086 (92%)

Sources of Supply: Limestone springs in River Witham valley and at Stroxton

Yield from Sources: Up to 3,000,000 gallons per day could be obtained

Filtration: 450 galls per sq. yd per day (each filter is 720 sq. yds)

Reservoir Storage: Saltersford: 7,250,000 + 400,000 galls; Spittlegate: 800,000 galls

Quantity Supplied: Daily average at 900,000 gallons; the supply is constant

Quality of Water: Good, total hardness levels at 13.23 degrees (high)

Water Pressure: Sufficient

The reservoir storage noted above does not include the additional 1,100,000 gallons constructed in the 1920s. Also, the 'Yield from Sources' seems high and perhaps does not reflect the minimum yields from the spring sources at times of low rainfall. It is noted that at the time of the return over 90% of the town's population was connected directly to the watermains network. It is presumed that those not directly connected would still be carrying their drinking water from the fountains or collection points provided for public use throughout the town.

It seems that construction work was occurring at Saltersford during the period between 1914 and 1918 even though it was the time of the First World War. A large army camp had been established at Belton Park immediately to the north of the

Town in 1915 at which up to 16,000 men were based. A water supply of up to 70,000 gallons per day was requested by the War Ministry to serve the camp.[33]

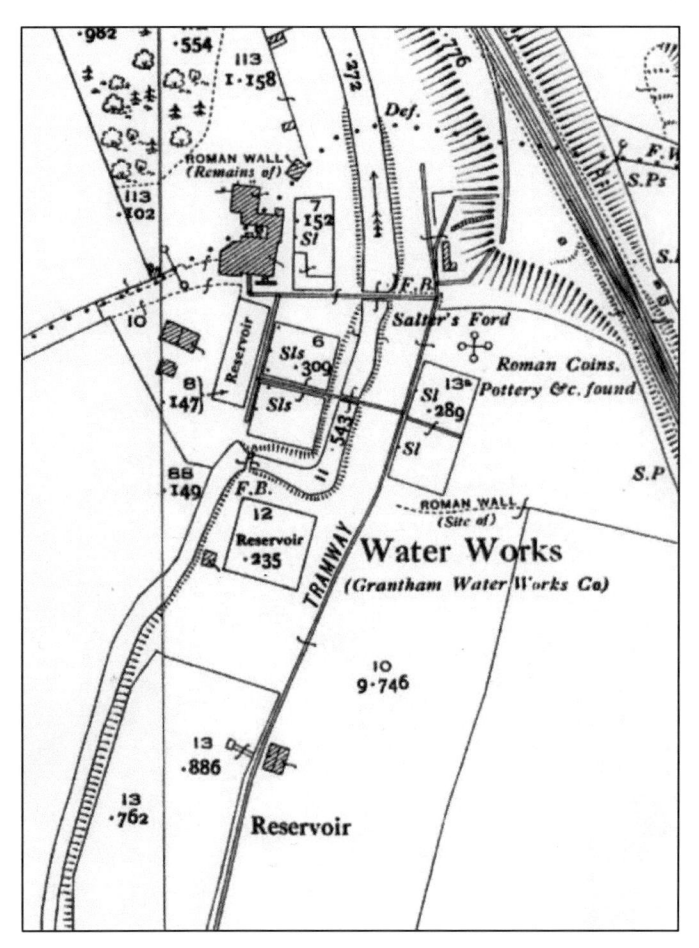

In the mid-1920s two new covered treated water tanks (750,000 and 350,000 gallons) were constructed. Water from the bankside springs at Little Ponton was piped direct into one, thus increasing the total storage for treated water at Saltersford to 1,500,000 gallons. From the Ordnance Survey map of 1929, it is interesting to see there was a tramway running down the length of the works on the east side of the river at Saltersford. The layout of the treatment works and pumping station at Saltersford in the late 1920s is shown to the left.

Saltersford in the 1920s. (Extract from Ordnance Survey County Series, 1:2500).

Because of the increased flows, the pipeline from the reservoir at Spittlegate was replaced with a larger 12-inch diameter pipe. The expansion of the watermains network within the town was taking place throughout the late 1800s and early 1900s, laying pipelines to individual homes and collection points. It is reported that watermains were being laid on both sides of the streets so to minimise the lengths of service pipes to individual homes. Virtually all mains pipes laid at this time were in cast iron with lead-run joints; service pipes laid to houses were of lead or galvanised iron.

---

[33] *GJ*, 6 February 1915.

During 1929 cracks were noticed in the side wall on the east side of the large settling tank. Expert advice was sought which concluded that movement had occurred within the embankment immediately above the tank.[34] Arrangements were hastily made to remove a large volume of the earth bank to relieve the superimposed load and to partially backfill the tank along the length of the east wall. This would increase its stability by reducing the depth of water along the east side by 50%. This also resulted in a small reduction of the tank capacity.

Saltersford Raw Water Lagoon (emptied).

By the 1930s the old 800,000-gallon covered brick service reservoir on Spittlegate Hill was deemed to be of insufficient size and elevation to supply the expanding watermains network. It was also said to be 'in a decayed condition'. This resulted in a new concrete reservoir being constructed on a ridge south of the town at nearby Gorse Lane. More than 30,000 'impervious concrete blocks' with steel reinforcement were used in the erection of the reservoir walls, an unusual method of construction. It is reported that all work on the design and construction was undertaken by the company's own staff and workforce under the supervision of their engineer, A.E.Musgrave. The capacity of the new reservoir was 1,000,000 gallons, with provision for another two similar sized reservoirs on the same site at a later date. An article published in the *Grantham Journal* in August 1935 reported that

---

[34] *GJ*, 9 February 1929.

instrumentation for recording water levels was to be installed and linked by telephone to the pumping station at Saltersford.[35] It was said that up to then a telescope had been used to observe water levels in the old Spittlegate reservoir from Saltersford, more than one mile away, which was 'not satisfactory in foggy weather'! In August 1936 the new reservoir was officially opened by Christopher Turnor, who had given much support to the Waterworks Company over several years.

With the construction of the new service reservoir on the ridge at Gorse Lane, a 140 bhp electrically-driven horizontal spindle-pump unit with an output of 100,000 galls per hour (2,400,000 gals/day) was supplied by Worthington Simpson of Newark and installed at Saltersford The new unit provided an alternative and more efficient means of pumping than the two existing oil-driven pumps; it had an output more or less the equivalent of both oil-driven pumps combined. With the threat of a war, the company had resolved to become less reliant on oil as a source of energy. At the same time, a pipeline was laid direct to the new reservoir on Gorse Lane from the newly installed electrically driven pump and the old pipeline to Spittlegate Hill was abandoned.

Even though the new reservoir was situated on higher ground, problems of low pressures and the maintenance of a constant supply were still being experienced in some of the higher areas of the town and on the fringe of the distribution network. To overcome the immediate problems, new booster stations were commissioned in 1937 on Barrowby High Road for the village of Barrowby and on Harrowby Lane for new housing development in uphill Harrowby. Both stations had duplicate pumping units installed and operated unmanned.[36]

However, the problems of maintaining a constant supply to the high-level areas to the west of the reservoir on Gorse Lane were still not totally resolved. Elevated storage was required. So, as part of the overall project, a reinforced concrete water tower was constructed on Gorse Lane to improve pressures and balance out the diurnal fluctuating demands for water by consumers. The tower has a capacity of 100,000 gallons and stands about 40 feet above ground level to the west of the service reservoir on Gorse Lane. A pumping unit was installed at the 1 Mg. service reservoir to lift water up to the water tower. The work was completed and put into use in 1939.

---

[35] *GJ*, 3 August 1935; an article entitled '£15,000 Waterworks Project'.
[36] *GJ*, 8 August 1936; a full-page article 'Developing Grantham's Water Supply'.

Gorse Lane Water Tower, 1949 and 2021.

Because the new service reservoir on Gorse Lane was at a higher elevation than the old Spittlegate Hill reservoir, all water taken from the springs at Stroxton needed to be diverted by a pipeline down to Saltersford and then pumped with the other waters to the new reservoir. However, with plentiful supplies from the Cringle Brook, the springs at Stroxton, with their unreliable yields during dry periods, were becoming of lesser importance as a water resource. In 1937 the average daily amount of water supplied by the company was 905,000 gallons.[37]

---

[37] *GJ*, 15 February 1938.

Water Supply in Wartime, 1939 to 1945

With the onset of war in 1939 it was necessary for the company to make safeguards to protect the flow of potable water to the town's inhabitants and manufacturing industries. Critical points in the water supply system were identified and precautions made against aerial bombing and sabotage.

Saltersford was declared a 'prohibited area' and was patrolled twenty-four hours every day throughout the years of the war. The operational pumping plant at Saltersford was located in a single tall brick pumphouse building and was considered vulnerable. As an emergency measure, a lorry-mounted diesel-driven pump unit with a pumping capacity of 1,000,000 gallons per day was purchased. This was housed in the old pumphouse on the east side of the river previously occupied by the Blake steam engine and could readily be connected into the pipe system supplying the Gorse Lane reservoir. As a mobile unit, it could also be used in an emergency within the town by taking water from an old well at there for direct abstraction from the River Witham.

Another vulnerable point in the system, for both water supply and railway, was where the pipelines supplying the town from service reservoir on Gorse Lane crossed over the main railway line at Spittlegate. Here twin 12-inch diameter pipes were attached to the main girders of the road bridge. The solution was to provide an alternative means of supply into the town by laying a new pipeline from Gorse Lane down Kitty Briggs Lane and connecting this to the watermains network on Harlaxton Road. The project was completed in October 1940 and water was soon flowing down the new pipeline to Harlaxton Road. On 7 November 1940 Spittlegate Bridge was bombed and the principal supply-line to the town destroyed. However, with the availability of the alternative pipeline down Kitty Briggs Lane, there was minimal disruption to water supplies in the town. It was a close call; calamity was averted by the fortuitous planning by those in charge.

At a meeting of the board in February 1941 it was reported that 'all water supplied by the company was now chlorinated against any harmful bacteria, with ammonia being pre-dosed prior to chlorine being added'. Also, that 'no complaints of taste had been received from consumers'.[38]

---

[38] *GJ*, 21 February 1941. All water supplies are now chlorinated. Ammonium sulphate is added after the dosage of chlorine to dechlorinate the water so reducing taste problems but still maintaining chlorine residuals in waters supplied.

Twin Vertical Spindle Pumps, installed at Saltersford, 1942

With the increase in wartime activities in 1942, additional water supplies were requested by the Air Ministry for the nearby RAF bases at Bottesford, Saltby and Harlaxton. To meet these additional needs, a new pumphouse was built on the roof of the largest of the three treated-water reservoirs at Saltersford, after the roof had been strengthened to take the additional loading. Being sited furthest away from the main pumphouse, the work afforded additional security in the event of aerial bombardment. Two 100 bhp electrically driven vertical-spindle pump units, supplied by Sulzers of Leeds, were installed with their pumps immersed in the reservoir waters below (see above). The combined output of the two pumps was 96,000 galls/hr (2,300,000 galls/day). A temporary pipeline was also laid direct from the water tower on Gorse Lane to supply RAF Bottesford.

The following year there was a drought and, in order to meet the needs of the Air Ministry while maintaining water supplies to the town, the company sought powers to abstract water direct from the river at Saltersford under the Defence Regulations.[39] Surprisingly, a number of objections were lodged, including those from the county and town councils, which resulted in a Public Enquiry being held in

---

[39] Defence Regulations 1939. Emergency regulations passed at the outbreak of the Second World War, which included powers to undertake work to maintain essential supplies, including water supplies.

the Guildhall in June 1943. The objectors were over-ruled and the company was given powers to abstract from the River Witham at Saltersford up to a maximum of 400,000 gallons per day, with the proviso that the water abstracted was treated. Fortunately, there was no cause for the implementation of these emergency powers for the remaining period of the war.

At the time of the Enquiry work had already started on the construction of a bank of filters to treat water abstracted direct from the river at Saltersford. A new building, close by the new pumphouse, was to house six rapid gravity filters that could treat up

Saltersford Filter & Pump House (above and to the left).

to 2 million gallons per day. The cleaning process for the old sand filters was slow and labour intensive, whereas that for the new rapid gravity filters was much quicker, more efficient and required less manpower. Soon the sand filters, capable of filtering only 1 million gallons per day, would become redundant. In 1944 the average daily amount of water supplied by the company was 1.82 million gallons, of which up to 30% was to the local RAF bases.[40]

---

[40] Waterworks Centenary booklet.

The Post-War Years, 1945 to 1961

At the board meeting of directors in August 1945, immediately following the end of hostilities, the company's manager F.A. Gibson, was able to give a full account of work undertaken during the previous six years in maintaining water supplies to the town. Reporting publicly on such matters was prohibited during the war years, especially the bomb damage in Spittlegate in November 1940.

The drought year of 1943 had made those in charge aware of just how limited and vulnerable the company's water resources were. More raw water storage was required to maintain flows during the dry periods. It was decided to utilise the ornamental lakes on the Cringle Brook at Stoke Rochford. These had silted up over the years but, by dredging and constructing new dams, raw water storage capacity was increased. In 1945 a 999-year lease was granted by Major Turnor to the company for the lakes and a strip of land around their edges on which work could be undertaken and water abstracted.

Easton Embankment Dam.

Improvements were made to the existing dams and weirs, including the reconstruction of the concrete dam at Thunder Bridge on the lowest lake. Together with improvements made on the Easton dam, one mile upstream of Stoke Rochford Hall, raw water storage on the lakes was substantially increased. This safeguarded supplies by maintaining a flow of water direct to Saltersford during periods of low natural flows in the Cringle Brook. These works were completed by 1950. By this time the average daily amount of water supplied by the company had fallen back to 1.3 million gallons due in part to the reduced supplies to the RAF bases in peacetime.[41] The town's population in 1951 was 23,555.

In 1948 the Ministry of Health required a report to be prepared for the 'surveying of water supplies and resources for large areas with common interests' in England. C.H.Spens MICE, a Ministry Inspector, was directed to undertake the survey for the area identified as 'Lincolnshire (Parts Lindsey and Kesteven) and North Nottinghamshire'.[42] As part of the work, population growth and future water supply requirements were to be estimated together with a programme of work prepared to meet the increased needs and existing shortfalls. The report would cover much of the county of Lincolnshire, including a large number of water undertakings from Grimsby in the north to Lincoln, as well as nearby Sleaford and Grantham.

The Grantham Waterworks Company's area of supply was included with the rest of west Kesteven and was identified as a 'dry area with few water resources'. For Grantham Borough the increase in population was estimated to rise from 22,260 in 1948 to 30,000 in 1970, with a corresponding increase in water requirements from the current 1.4 million gpd to 2.7 million gpd in the same period, nearly a two-fold increase.

At the time of the report by Spens, reliable yields from the total water resources supplying Grantham were assessed at only 1.77 million gpd, comprising 1.0 million gpd from the Cringle Brook intake at Stoke, 0.3 million gpd from the Witham springs, 0.07 million gpd from the Stroxton springs and 0.4 million gpd as an emergency or temporary supply direct from the River Witham at Saltersford. A new water resource for Grantham was urgently required.

The main recommendation for Grantham was to develop a new water resource in the limestones near Lenton, 7 miles south-east of the town. This took account of the work being undertaken at that time in improving raw water storage at Stoke Rochford and the yield from the Stoke Rochford intake. Water abstracted at Lenton would be pumped via a new pipeline to a service reservoir to be constructed at

---

[41] *GJ*, 14 March 1952.
[42] The Report entitled 'Water Supply Survey Lincolnshire (Parts Lindsey & Kesteven) & North Nottinghamshire) was commissioned by the Ministry of Health in 1948 and prepared by C.H. Spens M.I.C.E. one of the Ministry's Inspectors. It was concerned with 'surveying of water supplies and resources of large areas with common interest'.

Harrowby Top to provide a supply and storage on the north side of the town. Also included was the formation of a larger water undertaking called 'Kesteven Water' which would include the town of Sleaford and much of the surrounding rural area. This would improve operational efficiency and spread out available manpower resources. Looking back, the recommendations made by Spens were to a large degree implemented during the subsequent years.

In 1949 the Waterworks Company celebrated the centenary of its formation. A booklet which reviewed the past hundred years of the company was prepared for presentation to the board of directors.[43] It included a number of old photographs. The contents of the Centenary Booklet have been a valuable source of information in the preparation of this paper.

During the 1950s exploratory work was ongoing in finding an additional source of water to supply Grantham from the Lincolnshire limestone aquifer to the east of the escarpment, as recommended by Spens in his report of 1948. Exploratory boreholes were drilled during 1953 in the Lenton area, as suggested by Spens, but these proved to be of low yield. Other sites would subsequently be explored with the drilling of boreholes and test-pumping.

Following the decommissioning of the many RAF bases throughout the country, the Waterworks Company made a payment to the Air Ministry for the plant and watermains that had been installed by the Ministry during the war years at bases within their area of supply, such as RAF Bottesford. This complied with the new Water Act of 1945 and, in the case of Grantham, cost the company more than £7,000.[44] These were temporary installations for wartime needs and required much maintenance for longer term use. It is not clear whether the Waterworks Company welcomed taking on the responsibility for this hastily installed wartime infrastructure.

In November 1953 a notice was posted in the *Grantham Journal* announcing increases in the domestic water rate, based on the rateable value of properties ranging from £5 to £100 for houses with a water closet and one bath.[45] For a property with a rateable value of £50 the fixed charge was to be increased to £1/-/5d, and to £2/-/- for a house with a rateable value of £100.

---

[43] Centenary of the Grantham Waterworks Company, 1849 -1949 Booklet.
[44] Water Act 1945. This brought together previous water legislation and introduced a waterworks code. It also provided powers to construct works and lay watermains.
[45] *GJ*, 6 November 1953.

In 1954, under the powers provided under the Water Act 1945, the company sought authority to raise £25,000 for the construction of a new service reservoir on Gorse Lane and to repeal the two Grantham Waterworks Acts of 1873 and 1909. Construction on the reservoir started in March 1957 and was completed later in the year. The reservoir, which still sits at the highest point on Gorse Lane at the top of Kitty Briggs Lane, is circular and constructed in pre-stressed concrete with a capacity of 1.0 million gallons. The provision of the new reservoir increased total uphill capacity to 2.1 million gallons, which was well in excess of the 1956 daily consumption of 1.47 million gallons.[46]

Circular Reservoir (white structure in centre background) on Gorse Lane.

The two service reservoirs and the water tower on Gorse Lane are shown on the plans on pages 21 and 47. For reasons of clarity, the rectangular reinforced concrete reservoir constructed in 1937 is shown as Reservoir 1 and the circular prestressed concrete reservoir constructed in 1957 is shown as Reservoir 2. The tall concrete water tower constructed in 1938 lies between the two reservoirs on Gorse Lane and the cutting of the Grantham (A1) Bypass comes between the tower and Reservoir 2.

By this time, the company was providing bulk supplies of water to a number of the outlying villages around the town that came within the jurisdiction of the West Kesteven Rural District Council, who were responsible for providing water supplies to the rural areas around Grantham. These villages included Great Gonerby,

---

[46] *GJ*, 14 March 1958.

Barrowby, Harlaxton, Bottesford, Saltby, Allington and Long Bennington, with negotiations in hand to provide bulk supplies to other villages in the area.

Major road works were being undertaken during 1959 with the construction of the A1 Grantham Bypass. The route of the bypass is on the west side of the town, with a deep cutting across the line of the Gorse Lane ridge. The result was that the two service reservoirs and water tower on Gorse Lane would be separated by the 23-feet-deep road cutting with a need to relay the interconnecting watermains.[47] This was achieved by incorporating two new pipelines within the structure of the new Gorse Lane road bridge that spans the deep road cutting. The water tower on Gorse Lane now literally towers over the A1 on the eastern edge of the road cutting and is clearly visible to traffic passing below.

There was another drought during 1959, which resulted in serious water shortages despite the work some ten years earlier on the Stoke Park lakes. A hosepipe ban was implemented together with a ban on all non-essential water use. The shortage of water would not have been helped by the excessive leakage from the pipe network inherited from the RAF on their base at Bottesford.[48]

During the late 1950s discussions continued with the neighbouring water undertakers with a view to implementing the recommendations made by Spens for regrouping and forming one large water undertaking for the Grantham and Sleaford area. The Grantham Waterworks Company was broadly in favour of the proposal but the Grantham Borough Council was not so enthusiastic, suggesting that an even larger area should be considered.

In compliance with the recommendations of the Water Act 1945, many other water undertakings throughout England were in similar discussions at the time with the objective of forming larger, more efficient joint water boards with board members representing the local areas supplied.[49] However, the formation of a new Kesteven Water Board would have meant the demise and dissolution of the Grantham Waterworks Company. Nevertheless, with limited water resources and the need to find finance for a new water source, pipeline and reservoir, it was perhaps not a difficult decision. Shareholders would surely be compensated.

---

[47] *GJ*, 13 April 1959.
[48] *GJ*, 2 October 1959. 500,000-gallon leak found at RAF Bottesford.
[49] Water Act 1945'.

The Kesteven Water Board, 1961 to 1974

Following consultations with neighbouring water undertakings and local councils and under the powers conferred under a Special Parliamentary Order, the new Kesteven Water Board was formed in 1961. The new board would be responsible for the supply and distribution of drinking water to the towns of Grantham and Sleaford together with the rural districts of West and East Kesteven. This resulted in the dissolution of the Grantham Waterworks Company, whose assets were transferred to the new water board.

Kesteven Water Board Offices in Finkin Street.

The Board's offices would be based in Grantham using the former company's offices on Finkin Street and retaining most of the company's staff. Under the national reorganisation of water utilities, North Kesteven Rural District would come under the jurisdiction of the new Lincoln and District Water Board, whilst South Kesteven would be served by the new South Lincolnshire Water Board based in Spalding.

Although much improvement work had been undertaken by the rural district councils during the 1950s by providing, often for the first time, piped water supplies to many villages, one of the top priorities of the new water board was to continue with this work in the rural areas. Another priority was to develop a new water source for the Borough of Grantham, whose population continued to grow. In addition, a large food processing complex was soon to be established at Easton, near Colsterworth which required a large supply of water each day. With the output from Saltersford near the top limit, a new source of water was certainly required. Following the successful test-pumping of exploratory boreholes into the Lincolnshire limestones at Aswarby, a licence was obtained to abstract on average 1.0 Mgd (4.5 Mld) up to a maximum of 2.0 Mg (9.09 Ml) on any one day.[50]

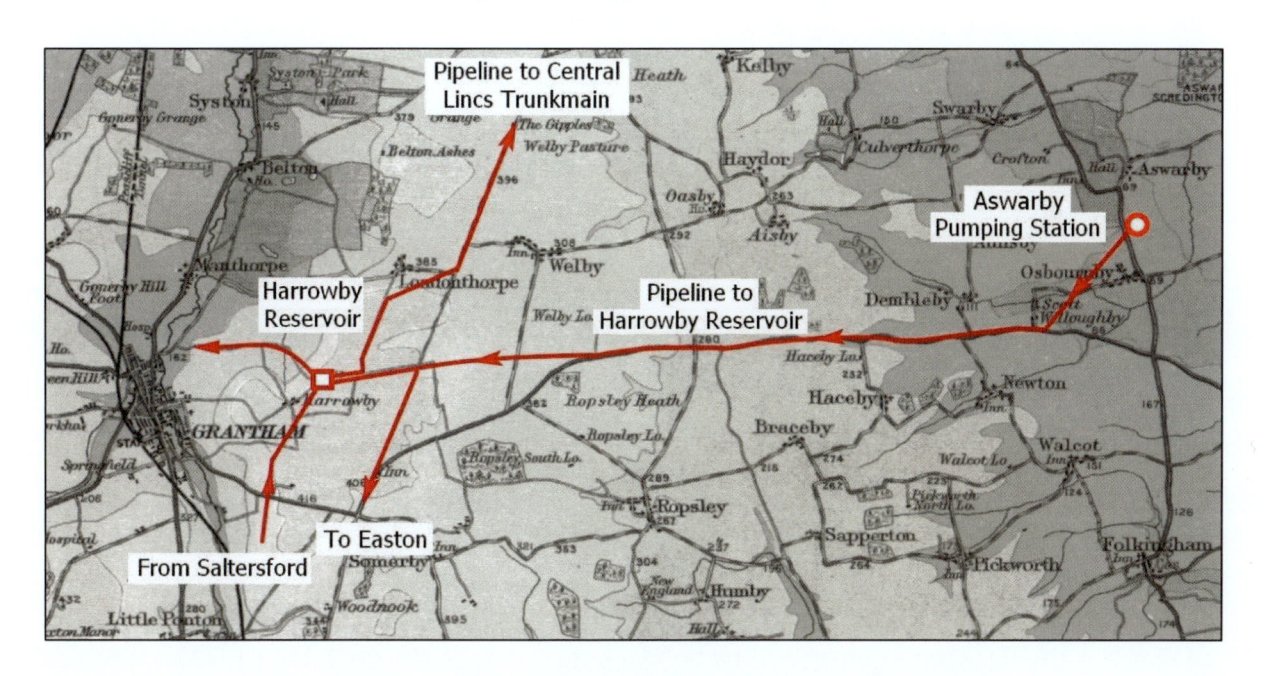

Grantham Water Supplies, from Aswarby Pumping Station.

Work soon commenced on the development of this source of water with the construction of a new pumping station alongside the A15 between Aswarby and Osbournby, together with the laying of a 20-inch (500 mm)^2 diameter pipeline about 8 miles (13 kms) in length following the A52 for most of the way to Harrowby Top.

---

[50] Licence to Abstract' from two boreholes in the Lincolnshire Limestone at Aswarby, 1,659,320 cu. m./year with a maximum of 9,092 cu.m. on any one day.

Here a new 2.0 Mg (9 Ml) capacity covered service reservoir was constructed from which water supplies would gravitate to the northern part of Grantham.

As part of the planning permission given for the new pumphouse at Aswarby, it was agreed that the external walls of the building be constructed in the local limestone so as to blend in with surrounding buildings in the area. Following its construction, it was difficult to identify the building as a pumping station. Work on the new scheme was completed in 1970, thus providing an extra and alternative supply of water to supplement that provided over the years from Saltersford.

Harrowby Top service reservoir.

The top water level of the new service reservoir at Harrowby Top (412.00 feet (125.60 m) AOD) was engineered to be the same as that of the 1 Mg (4.5 Ml) circular pre-stressed concrete reservoir on Gorse Lane that had been completed in 1957. This was with the intention of connecting the two reservoirs in the future with a ring main to enable both reservoirs to operate in conjunction with each other in serving the northern and western areas of the town and outlying villages. In 1974 a new 18-inch (450-mm) diameter ring-main was laid around the western and northern perimeters of Grantham connecting up these two high-level reservoirs. (See map on facing page.)

During the 1960s there was much talk of adding fluoride to water supplies. The Royal College of Physicians published a report recommending the addition of fluoride in water supplies to bring levels up to 1.0 mg/litre to reduce the decay of children's teeth and to prevent dental caries throughout life. It was a hotly debated issue, and it was left to each local Health Authority to decide whether to request the local water undertakings to fluoridise water supplies in their areas. All costs associated with the adding of fluoride would be paid by the local Health Authority.

The local Health Authority in Kesteven was in favour of such measures and subsequently requested the water board to proceed with the necessary work. The Kesteven Water Board was one of the first water undertakings in England to add fluoride to their water supplies. It installed a proto-type plant at its Ashby Pumping Station which controlled the dilution and dosage of the hydro-fluorosilicic acid. Similar equipment was later installed at both Saltersford and Aswarby.

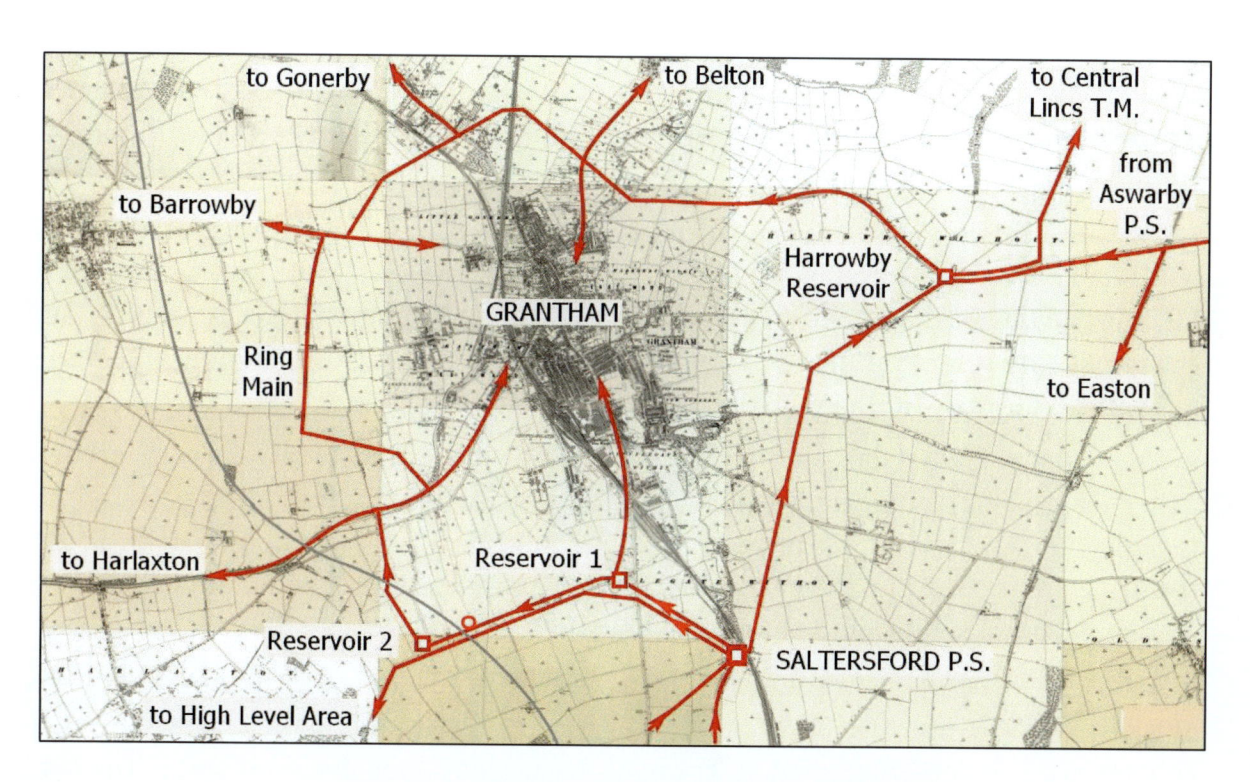

Grantham Water Supplies: Pipe Network in the Town.

Anglian Water Authority, 1974 to 1989

In 1973 a new Water Act was passed that was to create ten regional water authorities for England and Wales.[51] The new authorities would be responsible for water supply and sewerage services together with water conservation, land drainage and flood control. The whole of Lincolnshire would come under the control of the new Anglian Water Authority which would have its headquarters based in Huntingdon. Within the Anglian Authority, five divisions based on river catchment areas would be created, based in Lincoln, Oundle, Norwich, Cambridge and Colchester.

Initially, each division contained three separate functional divisions for water supply, sewerage and river management / land drainage. The new water division covering Grantham would be based in Lincoln and be known as the Lincoln Water Division of Anglian Water, encompassing the five former water boards based at Grimsby, Scunthorpe, Skegness, Lincoln and including the Kesteven Water Board at Grantham.

The implementation of the new organisation took place on 1 April 1974, with head-office staff transferring from Grimsby, Scunthorpe, Skegness and Grantham to Lincoln. However, the day-to-day operations of the pumping stations, reservoirs and the pipe networks continued to be supervised from the local depots, including Saltersford for the Grantham area.

One of the advantages of the larger authority was the availability of greater expertise in the planning and distribution of water resources over a wider area. This included the transfer of water resources and supplies across the boundaries of the former water boards. In 1984 Lincoln's three separate single-function divisions were combined into a single multi-functional Lincoln Division.

In 1976 there was a prolonged drought with minimal rainfall throughout the autumn of 1975 and the early part of 1976 and water supplies across the entire country were severely affected. A 'Drought Emergency' was declared and a 'Drought Minister' appointed. With little snow or rainfall during the preceding autumn and winter months to recharge the local limestone aquifer, the springs feeding the Cringle Brook and River Witham had virtually dried up.

---

[51] Water Act 1973. Under this Act ten regional water authorities were formed in England & Wales who were responsible for water resources, water supply, sewerage services, water conservation, land drainage and flood control – subject to government targets and financial control.

As an emergency measure, a 600mm diameter pipeline was laid alongside the A1 highway from Empingham Reservoir (now Rutland Water) across the watershed to Colsterworth to allow the transfer of up to 32 Ml per day of water from the recently built and still only partly filled reservoir into the headwaters of the River Witham.[52] The work in laying the 19 km of pipeline was completed in less than 12 weeks.

Laying a water pipeline alongside the A1 from Rutland Water in 1976.

The transfer of raw water from Rutland Water maintained the flows in the Witham that had been depleted by the drought and the drying up of springs. This in turn allowed water to be abstracted direct from the River Witham further downstream at Saltersford by the installation of temporary pumping plant.

The drought of 1976 ended in September of that year although it would be some time before the limestone springs started to flow again. Nevertheless, with other temporary measures in place including a ban on the use of water for non-essential use, water supplies to the town were maintained throughout the period of the drought.

In this same year, a study was made by Anglian Water of the short- and long-term needs for the supply of drinking water to central Lincolnshire covering an area from Grantham to Lincoln. The ability of the drought emergency works to supplement the

---

[52] Transfer of raw water from Rutland Water to the River Witham and Saltersford, undertaken by the Lincoln River Division of Anglian Water (now Environment Agency).

flows in the River Witham made Saltersford a key location in the overall planning strategy. With proper treatment to ensure drinking water standards were met, raw water transferred from Rutland Water to the River Witham and then abstracted at Saltersford could be used to meet future water supply demands for central Lincolnshire, including the Grantham, for years to come.

The main recommendations of the study were:

- The redevelopment of Saltersford treatment works and pumping station to produce up to 25 Mld (25,000,000 litres per day) by 1982.

- The laying of a trunk main between Grantham and Lincoln, 33 kms in length, connecting Saltersford treatment works in Grantham with the Bracebridge Heath service reservoir south of Lincoln. The new trunk main would also connect with other service reservoirs and water supply systems along its route. This work was also to be completed by 1982.

- The further development of the central limestone aquifer during the late 1980s, subject to the results obtained from current ground water investigations.

The general layout of the proposed central Lincolnshire water supply scheme that stretches from Grantham up to Lincoln and includes the Sleaford area is shown in the map on the facing page. Those aspects concerning work at Saltersford and the water supply to Grantham are described in the next section.

Saltersford Treatment Works Redevelopment, 1980 to 1983

In line with the recommendations of the study completed in 1977, work soon got underway on the planning and design of the new water treatment works and pumping station at Saltersford. In April 1980 contracts were let to French Kier Construction Ltd (civil engineering and building work), Degremont Laing Ltd (design and installation of the treatment plant) and Sulzer (UK) Ltd (supply and installation of the pumping plant). The works were designed for treating up to a maximum of 25 Mld of waters taken from the Cringle Brook, River Witham and from Rutland Water.

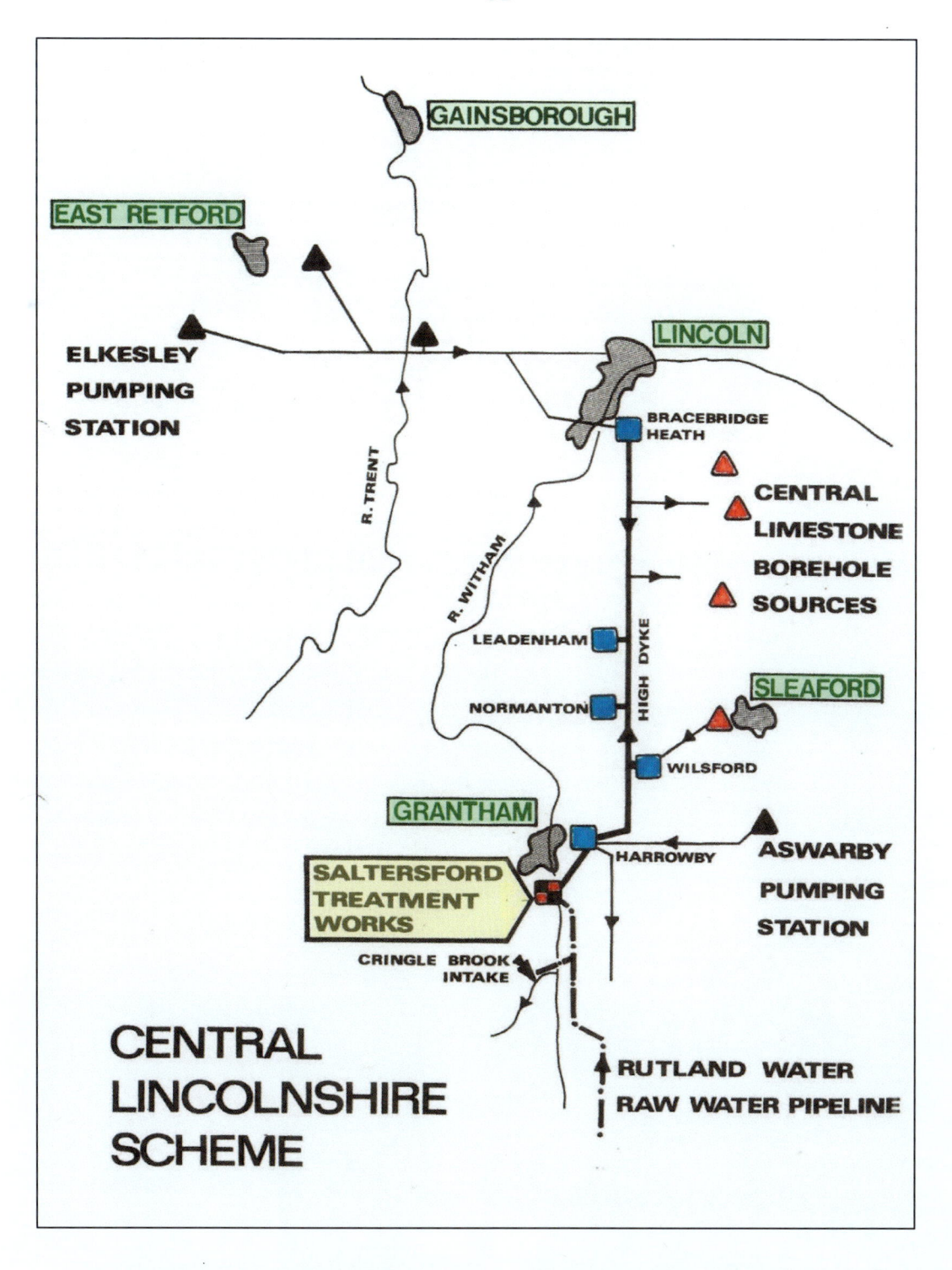

Central Lincolnshire water supply scheme, completed by Anglian Water in 1983

Saltersford Treatment Works, ground plan, 1983

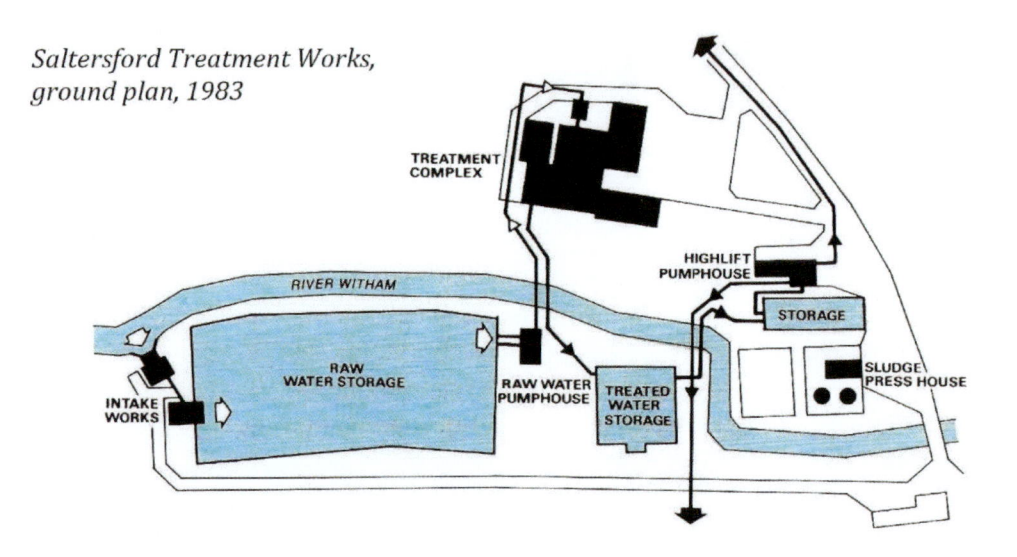

The raw water pipeline from Rutland Water was extended by another 11 km along the A1 highway to Saltersford Treatment Works. This latter measure was considered necessary to safeguard against accidental spillage and pollution of the River Witham from vehicles travelling on the heavily trafficked trunk road. A similar measure was undertaken later in 1988 when a new intake was constructed at the Thunder Bridge dam on the Cringle Brook and a pipeline laid form the new intake direct to Saltersford, thus bypassing the existing intake at Stoke, which is sited immediately below the A1 trunk road. This was new pipeline was to be for emergency use only.

*Saltersford:
New Treatment Works, 1983.*

The layout of the new works at Saltersford, as constructed in 1983, is shown above. At the top of the works (i.e. at the southerly end), is an intake from the river from which water is pumped to a cascade which then discharges into the old 32 Ml (7 Mg) raw water lagoon. Also piped to the top of the cascade as separate streams, are waters piped from the Cringle Brook and direct from Rutland Water. Water taken from the springs at Little Ponton continue to flow direct into the raw water lagoon, but the Stroxton Springs are no longer used.

Low-lift pumps deliver water from the raw water lagoon to a mixing tank at the head of the treatment works complex. Here chemicals are added to assist with the treatment process. The flow is then divided into three streams so to allow operational flexibility, passing first through three clarifiers (super pulsators) for settlement of the larger particles and then to six anthracite and sand rapid gravity filters to remove the finer particles. Chlorine and fluoride are then added prior to the water entering the treated-water reservoirs for which the two existing 3.4 and 2.5 Ml capacity tanks are used in tandem. Part of the process is the treatment of the sludge generated from the clarifiers which, when thickened, is pressed into a dry cake for disposal.

Saltersford: Raw Water Lagoon.

Five high-lift pump units supplied by Sulzer (UK) Ltd and driven by 97kW Lawrence Scott thyristor-controlled variable-speed D.C. motors are housed in a separate high-lift pumphouse building together with a 400 kva diesel-driven generator to provide emergency power sufficient for half the output of the works. From Saltersford water is pumped to the service reservoirs at Gorse Lane and Harrowby; the latter feeds the central Lincolnshire trunk main running to Lincoln.

A new pipeline was required to transfer water from Saltersford direct to Harrowby Reservoir on the high land to the north-east of the town. On leaving the treatment works, the pipeline crosses a cutting of the East Coast main railway line. To carry the pipeline over the cutting, an aluminium triodetic bridge was assembled on flat railway bogies in the railway sidings at Grantham station then transported by rail and lifted into position by a rail-mounted crane onto pre-constructed concrete abutments. The span between abutments is 34 metres. All work in lifting the pipe

Pipe Bridge over East Coast Main Railway Line.

bridge into position was undertaken during an eighteen-hour period of 'track possession' obtained from British Rail.

The project at Saltersford itself was completed and put into commission in May 1983 at a cost of £4.55M. The overall cost of the Central Lincolnshire Water Supply

Scheme was £8.51M.[53] The new works were officially opened by the Hon Douglas Hogg (at that time MP for Grantham) on the 15 July 1983. All work was project managed and supervised by Anglian Water's own engineering staff.

Prior to the construction work commencing at Saltersford, archaeological investigations were undertaken by the South Lincolnshire Archaeological Unit. Following the removal of topsoil over the site of the proposed treatment complex, various finds dating back to the time of the Roman settlement were exposed. These included a T-shaped grain drier, stone-lined pit – which contained evidence of burning – and a series of gullies leading into a stone-lined water-collecting tank[54] (see photograph opposite).

Since being commissioned in 1983, additional works have been carried out, such as the provision of GAC (granular activated carbon) pressure filters with ozone treatment in order to improve water quality and taste. A fish monitor was also installed to detect any deterioration in the quality of water taken direct from the River Witham, although this has subsequently been taken out of use.

Archaeological Excavation at Saltersford.

GAC pressure filters were also installed at Aswarby Pumping Station during the early 1990s to improve water quality. The exposed tall cylindrical steel vessels that contain the filter media have taken away some of the aesthetic value of the original pumping station with its original stone-built pumphouse building. A screen of trees has since been planted to soften the new features and mask the high security fencing which surrounds the site.

---

[53] Anglian Water's leaflet 'Saltersford Treatment Works'. The costs are given at November 1982 prices which equate respectively to £15M and £28M at 2020 prices.
[54] Lincs to the Past website - Romano-British Settlement, Saltersford - ref MLI33968.

Anglian Water Services Ltd, 1989 to 2000

Under the Conservative Government during the late 1980s most of the public utilities and services were privatised. The water industry did not escape and a Bill of Parliament was passed for the privatisation of all water authorities in England and Wales under the Water Act (Privatisation) (1989).[52] The Anglian Water Authority became a private limited company (plc) and renamed Anglian Water Services Ltd, now under the control of its shareholders, with shares being made available to both the public and employees under the provisions of the Act.

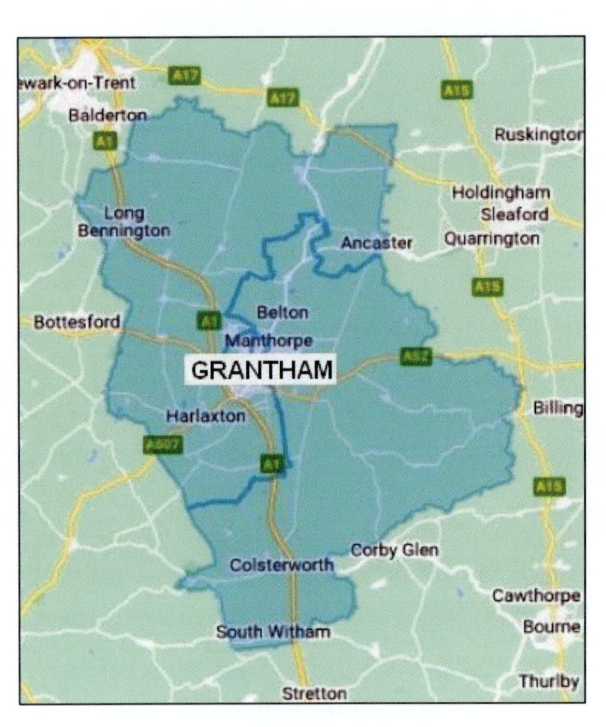

Grantham Water Supply Area.

The company was nevertheless regulated under the Water Industry Act 1991 to ensure that set levels of service were met and that the interests of consumers were protected. Initially under the surveillance of the Director General of Water Services and supported by the Office of Water Services (OFWAT), the 1991 Act gave powers to impose hefty fines on the new water companies for non-compliance with the new statutory standards.

Although there was a great deal of change at top management level, the day-to-day operation of the water supply undertaking saw little change at local level, apart from the inevitable measures of economy and staff reductions. Up to the end of the twentieth century there was still a Divisional Office based at Lincoln which covered the Grantham area and a local depot at Saltersford where both the water supply and distribution operatives and staff were based.

With combined waters taken from the Cringle Brook, River Witham and Rutland Water, the treatment works and pumping station at Saltersford continued to be the principal source of drinking water supply for Grantham and the surrounding areas. Water continued to be transferred up the 33 kms of the central Lincolnshire trunk main to Lincoln and points *en route*. In addition, water was still abstracted from the limestone boreholes at Aswarby, which continued to be pumped direct to Harrowby Service Reservoir supplying the northern part of the town and the rural areas to the east and south of Grantham.

At the turn of the century in 2000, a population of up to 70,000 in the western area of Kesteven received their water supplies from either Saltersford or Aswarby. The supply district included the town of Grantham and the large rural area of approximately 500 sq. kilometres (200 sq. miles) from South Witham in the south to Caythorpe and Claypole in the north, as shown on the map opposite. The zone supplied with treated water from Saltersford is shaded in dark blue and that with limestone water from Aswarby shaded in light blue.

Levels of Service and Water Quality

All water undertakings have target levels of service set as a standard for drinking water supplied. The three basic parameters are constancy of supply, water pressure and quality. Other service requirements relate to issues such as work undertaken and customer service.

Constancy of supply and water pressure are controlled by sufficient pumping capacity and water storage within the system in order to maintain water supplies to customers in the event of failures such as loss of power supplies and burst watermains. With the ability to transfer raw water from Rutland Water together with the current treated water reservoir storage at both Gorse Lane and at Harrowby Top and the flexibility in the watermains network, Grantham and district is well provided with public water supplies.

The quality of water delivered is pure and wholesome and conforms to the standards and parameters of the current Drinking Water Directive. The chemical analysis of treated waters from both sourceworks together with the accepted levels in the Drinking Water Directive are contained in the table on the following page. Although within the accepted levels, the limestone waters from the Aswarby boreholes are classified as very hard with those from Saltersford only as hard. Waters from both sources are disinfected with chlorine. At the request of the local health authority, fluoride is artificially added to raise levels to 1.00 mg/l F. Unlike some other parts of the county, there are currently no problems of high levels of nitrates (as NO₃) in the water.

Chemical Analysis of Water Supplied

Chemical Parameter with Chemical Symbols & Units (mg/l = milligrams /litre)	Legal Limit[1]	Water Supply Zones [2]	
		Grantham West from Saltersford	Grantham East from Aswarby
Hydrogen Ions: pH value	6.5 to 9.5	7.34	7.4
Colour: mg/l pts colour scale	20	< 0.34	< 0.73
Turbidity: NTUs [3]	4	< 0.1	0.12
Conductivity: µS/cm at 20°C[4]	2500	627	647
Alkalinity: mg/l CaCO₃	no limit set	130	225
Total Hardness: mg/l CaCO₃	no limit set	93.9	134.1
Chlorides: mg/l Cl	250	68.8	50.4
Fluorides[5]: mg/l F	1.5	0.82	0.92
Iron: mg/l Fe	0.20	< 0.01	< 0.01
Manganese: mg/l Mn	0.05	< 0.002	< 0.002
Nitrates: mg/l NO₃	50	15.3	23.1
Nitrites: mg/l NO₂	0.5	< 0.025	< 0.03
Potassium: mg/l K	no limit set	8.49	12.9
Sodium: mg/l Na	200	44	27.1
Sulphates: mg/l SO₄	250	111	105

Notes

1. The 'Legal Limits' are those set by the current 'Water Supply (Water Quality) Regulations (2016) which superseded the EU Drinking Water Directive albeit with similar set limits for water quality parameters.
2. The water quality data listed for the two supply zones has been taken from Anglian Water's web-site for the period January to September 2020 which contains chemical parameters (46), microbiological parameters (15) and levels of pesticides (5) for both Zones together with the legal limits set.
3. NTU is an abbreviation for 'Nephelometric Turbidity Units'.
4. µS/cm is an abbreviation for 'micro-Siemens per centimetre'.
5. Fluoride is added in water supplied to both Supply Zones to artificially raise levels to 1.00 mg/l. The value given is the natural level of fluoride in waters abstracted and prior to treatment.
6. Chlorine is added at both water sourceworks to disinfect water supplies. Ammonia is not added to chloraminate water supplied from either of the two sources (as at 2020).

Concluding Comments

These days we all expect a reliable supply of a good quality piped water, provided 24 hours per day and 52 weeks a year. It is only when there is a failure in the supply system, such as a burst watermain, that we realise just how much we depend on a service that is generally taken for granted.

When looking back over the past 150 years, we realise that many of our predecessors did not enjoy the convenience of a piped water supply direct into their own homes. Some had to carry water from wells or public standpipes, where the quality of the water would at times be suspect and had for drinking purposes to be boiled. It is interesting to learn how the supply of water to the local inhabitants has evolved over the years, leading to improvements in their health, hygiene and general well-being.

It is of course right that in the twenty-first century we should all enjoy a reliable good quality water supply piped into own homes. It is one of the basic needs for life and in maintaining good health. Much has been said about the potential shortfall in water supplies, especially in Lincolnshire, which is one of the driest areas of the country. With the expanding population and increased demands for water, economies need to be made in our water usage and in the reduction of waste.

Nevertheless, new sources of water supply will be required, and improvement works undertaken to meet future needs and to maintain water quality standards. It is reassuring at least to know that future water requirements are continually being assessed by professionals and plans being made to ensure that water continues to flow through our taps, even though at times the construction of new reservoirs and other capital works can be controversial.

A clean, fresh supply of drinking water is essential for life to exist. We should all be so grateful that this can be readily obtained by the turn of a tap. The current metered charge (in 2020) is 160 pence for 1,000 litres for water delivered to an individual's home; what better value for money can there be?

Timeline of Grantham Water Supplies

1597 – 1860	Water supplied by pipe from Greyfriars' Spring to Conduit House
1849 – 1850	Grantham Waterworks Company set up under the Waterworks Clauses Act 1847
1850 – 1851	Water from Stroxton Springs supplied by pipe to reservoir on Spittlegate Hill
1858 - 1860s	Springs near River Witham at Little Ponton piped to Saltersford
1873	Grantham Waterworks Act 1873 and new Company formed
1874 -1875	Intake at Stoke developed and pumping station and reservoir constructed at Saltersford
1876 / 1897	Cornish beam engine installed at Saltersford, later modified
1883 / 1898	Tangye and Blake steam engines installed at Saltersford
1904 – 1906	Akroyd oil engine installed at Saltersford and sand filters constructed
1909	Grantham Waterworks Act 1909; Company given powers to raise capital and construct works
1909 – 1920	Two Hornsby oil engines installed at Saltersford; raw water reservoir and slow sand filters constructed
mid 1920s	Two treated water reservoirs constructed at Saltersford
1929	East wall of raw water reservoir / lagoon at Saltersford stabilised
1936	Service reservoir at Gorse Lane completed; 140 HP W.S. pump installed at Saltersford; Spittlegate reservoir decommissioned
1937 – 1939	Water tower on Gorse Lane constructed and booster pumps installed for supplies to Barrowby and Harrowby Top
1939 – 1945	Two vertical spindle pump units installed at Saltersford; lorry mounted diesel pump purchased; emergency licence given to abstract water from the Witham; new pipeline laid down Kitty Briggs Lane
1946 – 1950	Stoke Park Lakes dredged and dams improved
1957 – 1959	A1 Grantham bypass built; second service reservoir constructed on Gorse Lane
1961	Kesteven Water Board formed and based at Grantham
1969 – 1974	New boreholes and pumping station commissioned at Aswarby and service reservoir constructed at Harrowby Top; Grantham ring-main created; fluoridation of water supplies introduced
1974	Anglian Water Authority formed with Divisional Offices in Lincoln
1976	Drought Year; pipeline laid from Rutland Water to Colsterworth
1980 – 1983	Saltersford Treatment Works redeveloped; pipeline laid to Harrowby Reservoir and Rutland Water pipeline extended to Saltersford
1988	New intake on Cringle Brook at Thunder Bridge constructed
1989 – 1994	Anglian Water plc formed; improvement works at Saltersford and Aswarby

Summary of Supply Systems

Table 1. Sourceworks

Sourceworks	Average Output Mgd	Average Output Mld	Max Output Mgd	Max Output Mld	Year Developed	Notes
Stroxton Springs	0.07	0.32	-----	-----	1851	flow to Spittlegate Reservoir
Witham Springs	0.30	1.36	-----	-----	1860s	flow to Saltersford
Cringle Brook	1.00	4.55	-----	-----	1874	flow to Saltersford
R Witham (temp)	0.40	1.82	0.40	1.82	1943	pumped to Gorse Lane
R Witham (new)	4.40	20.00	4.40	20.00	1983	trans from Rutland Water
Aswarby Boreholes	1.00	4.55	1.50	7.00	1980	pumped to Harrowby Reservr.

Mgd. – million gallons per day; Mld – million litres per day

Table 2. Pumping Equipment

Pumping Station	Manufacturer	Type	No.	Output (per unit) rating	g/h	l/h	Year Installed
Saltersford – s	'Grasshopper'	beam engine	1	20 HP	-----	-----	1874
Saltersford – s	Perran - Cornwall	beam engine	1	70 HP	42	190	1876
Saltersford – s	Blake & Knowles	recip' pump	1	----	----	----	1898
Saltersford – o	Hornsby & Sons	'Akroyd'	1	----	30	140	1902
Saltersford – o	Hornsby	H' Tyler pump	1	95 HP	40	180	1916
Saltersford – o	Ruston & Hornsby	Gwynne pump	1	110 HP	50	230	1918
Saltersford – e	Worthington Sim.	horiz. spindle	1	140 HP	100	460	1936
Saltersford – e	Sulzers of Leeds	vert. spindle	2	100 HP	48	220	1942
Saltersford	Sulzer (UK) Ltd	variable speed	5	97 kW	60	260	1983
Aswarby	British Pleuger	submersible	2	180 HP	52	238	1970

Table 3. Reservoirs

Reservoir	Capacity Mg	Capacity Ml	TWL-AOD ft	TWL-AOD m	Year Built	Construction
Spittlegate Hill	0.800	3.600	330	100	1851	brick with concrete base
Saltersford raw	7.250	33.000	203	62	1914	open - mass concrete walls
Saltersford 1	0.400	1.800	200	61	1898	mass concrete + blue brick walls
Saltersford 2	0.450	2.000	200	61	1920's	reinforced concrete
Saltersford 3	0.750	3,400	200	61	1920's	reinforced concrete
Gorse Lane 1	1.000	4.550	370	113	1936	concrete blocks + steel bars
Gorse Lane 2	1.000	4.550	422	126	1957	circular prestressed concrete
Gorse Lane Tower	0.100	0.455	460	140	1938	reinforced concrete
Harrowby Top	1.000	4.550	422	126	1970	reinforced concrete

Table 4. Population and Water Supplied

Year	Population (approx.)	Water Supplied Mgd	Water Supplied Mld
1100	1,000	-	-
1879	15,000	0.580	2.640
1911	20,070	0.900	4.100
1931	21,200	0.900	4.100
1937	21,500	0.905	4.118

Year	Population (approx.)	Water Supplied Mgd	Water Supplied Mld
1944	-	1.820	8.280
1948	22,260	1.400	6.370
1956	29,500	1.470	6.680
1971	46,700		
2001	68,000		

Index

A1 Grantham By-pass 42, 43
Akroyd engine 28, **29**,
Acts of Parliament 17, 22, 30, 41, 42, 48, 56
Anglian Water Authority 4, 48-55
Anglian Water Services Ltd 55-57
archaeology 12, 27, 55, **55**
Aswarby pumping station 45-47, **45**, 55, 57, 58, 60

Barrowby Beck 14
Barrowby booster station 34
Barrowby Road, Grantham 14
Barrowby village water supply 43
Bath Spring 8, **8**, 19
Belton Park 31
Blake steam pump 25, **25**, 36
boreholes 7, 41, 57
bridge over railway line 54, **54**

Causennae, Roman settlement 5, 12, 19, 27-28
Centenary of Waterworks Company 41
Central Lincolnshire Water Supply Scheme 54
chlorination 36, 53, 58
Conduit House 5, 14-15
Cornish beam engine 25, 29
Cornish boilers 24, 26
Cringle Brook 6, 8-11, 19-22, 29, 30, 35, 40, 48, 50, 52, 53, 56

Degremont Laing Ltd 50
Drinking Water Directive 57
drought conditions 37, 39, 43, 48-49

Easton embankment dam 11, 39
Easton food processing plant 45

filters 22, 27, 28-31, 38, 53, 55
fluoride additive 46-47, 53, 58
French Kier Construction Ltd 50

geology 6-8
Gibson, F A, Company Manager 39

Gorse Lane reservoir 1 (1930s) 33-36
Gorse Lane reservoir 2 (1950s) 42, **42**, 46, 54, 57
Gorse Lane water tower 34, **35**, 37, 42, 43
Grantham Maltings, well 36
Grantham Museum 5, 28,
Grantham ring main 46, **47**
Grantham Scientific Society 28
Grantham Waterworks Company 4, 17, 19, 20, 22, 26, 27, 31, 40, 41, 43
Grasshopper beam engine 22, 24, 25, 28
Great North Road 9, 20, 22
Great Northern Railway 15, 20
Greyfriars 5, 13-14

hand pumps 15
Harlaxton Road, Grantham 36
Harlaxton, water supply to 43
Harrowby Lane, booster station 34
Harrowby Top reservoir 40, 45-46, **46**, 54, 57
Haywood, water engineer 20
Haywood Tyler pump 28
Health Authority 47, 58
Hornsby, Richard & Sons, engineers 5, 26, 28-29
Hovel Spring 19

Kesteven Water Board 43, 44, 47, 48
Kitty Briggs Lane, pipeline 36, 42

Lancashire boiler 26
Lenton 40, 41
lias clay 7
Lincoln Water Division 48
Little Ponton 8, 17, 19, 32, 53

mains pipes 31-33, 36, 41, 57
Meredith, George, engineer 17
Ministry of Health 40
Musgrave, A E, engineer 33

nitrates 58

outputs 23, 28, 34, 37, 45, 54

Perran Foundry of Cornwall, 23
population 5, 6, 12, 15, 20, 31, 40, 45
Preston, Henry, manager 5n, 26-28, **27, 28**
Public Enquiry, 1943 37-38

RAF Bottesford 37, 41, 43
RAF Harlaxton 37
RAF Saltby 37
railway 15, 17, 20, 24, 25, 36, 54, **54**
Return of Water Undertakings 30
Roman period 5, 12-13, 19, 27-28, 55
Ruston & Hornsby engine 28-29, **29**
Rutland Water 49-50, 52, 53, 56, 57

Saltersford, Pumping Station 4, 11, 19-26, 28-50, 55-57
Saltersford, Roman settlement 5, 12, 13, 27-28
Settling tank 22, 30, 33
Sleaford 40, 41, 43, 44, 50
Spens, C H, Ministry Inspector 40-43
Spittlegate reservoir 17-19, **19**, 22, 32, 33-35
Spring Head 10, 11, **11**
steam engine pump
Stoke Rochford 6, 9-11, **9**, 20, 30, 39-40

Stroxton springs 8, 17-20, 24, 31, 35, 40, 53
Sulzer, Leeds, pump supplier 37, 50 54
Swamp Spring 19

Tangye, pump & engine supplier 24, 26
Teague, William, water engineer 26
Thompson's Yard 26
Thunder Bridge 11, **12**, 39, 52
trunk main 50, 52, 54, 57
Turnor, Christopher, of Stoke Rochford 20, 34
Turnor, Major H 39

water rate 41
waterfall 9, 11, **11**,
Waterworks Clauses Act (1847) 17
Welby, Sir Glynne, landowner 17
wells 12-13, 15, 27, 36, 59
West Kesteven Rural District Council 42
Witham, River 6-9, 12, 17, 20, 36, 38, 40, 49-50, 52, 55, 56
World War One 5, 31-32
World War Two 6, 36-38, 41
Worthington Simpson, Newark, 34
Wyville Beck 8

UNITS

In this book imperial units have been used for the period up to 1974 and metric units thereafter.

CONVERSIONS

1 gallon = 4.55 litres
1 inch = 25.4 mm
1 foot = 0.305 metres
1 mile = 1.61 kilometres
1 shilling = 5 pence

1 litre = 0.22 gallons
1 cm = 0.39 inches
1 metre = 3.28 feet
1 km = 0.621 miles
1 penny = 2.4 old pence

ABBREVIATIONS

bhp = brake house power
gph = gallons per hour
gpd = gallons per day
kVA = kilo volt-amperes
kw = kilowatts

Mg = million gallons
Mgd = million gallons per day
Ml = million or mega litres
Mld = million litres per day

Printed in Great Britain
by Amazon